wisdom

at wit's end

Printed in the United States of America
First Edition Printing, 2018

Published by Inkwell Book Co
Cover Photo Adobe Stock

www.LiaMartinWriting.com

ISBN-13   978-0-9977644-3-7

wisdom
at wit's end

abandoning
supermom myths
in search of
supernatural peace

lia martin

If any of you lacks wisdom,
you should ask God,
who gives generously to all
without finding fault,
and it will be given to you.

—James 1:5 (NIV)

table of contents

introduction

I tried rewriting this introduction so many times. Every time I reviewed the collection of words, I sensed my own fear. Every time, it felt like I was gently placing cartoon bandages on my wildly hemorrhaging heart.

I want to get real now. Real moms like you who have told me to are expecting it. I hope you want to get real, too. This book is my offering. It is what God has whispered to me for so long that it pounds in my soul like an earthquake.

Living has shown me what sort of mom I want to become. I'm betting the story of your life has shaped how you want to mother, too. Right away, I have to say that if you don't want to be a mom, don't find pleasure in being a mom, don't have a desire to enjoy your children—this book is not for you. This book is for moms who love being moms so much that we're driving ourselves to a sort of undefinable disintegration.

This book is a hand to hold if you, too, feel that the world's demands are so loud that you've unwittingly arrived at your wit's end. By copying others. By competing. By comparing, stressing, perfecting, and choosing what sometimes feels like failing.

By making you a mom, God offers the world-altering honor of shepherding lives other than your own. He also is the giver of free will to choose. How you live your life as a mom and how you lead your children into adulthood are your choices. I don't want us to forget that. Whoever or whatever has you in a state of stress over not being good enough is not good for you.

What I want is a renewal of your tendency to listen for God's guidance for you. Let me repeat that. *His* guidance. For *you*. Absolutely no one knows you and what you're going through better than the One who made you.

In my own journey from pregnancies to births, through pre-K, K through 12, and the heart-wrenching college send-off, I have linked arms, voices, and efforts with so many moms. Moms who've become lifelong girlfriends, valuable coworkers, mentors, and more. What I keep feeling that will no longer leave me alone is that moms are multitasking at such a breakneck speed that we're living in fear instead of faith. We're feeling such an incessant pressure to "Be more! Do more! Be intentional! Make it happen!" that we're effectively bypassing the sweetness of our short, original lives.

I guess you could say I have a heart for moms. You could also say I have a burden for speaking truth into our identities. I have led Bible study groups, attended women's conferences, and just plain sat next to mom after mom at practices, performances, sporting events, girls' nights out, and more while we're smack in the midst of serving as moms, wives, sisters, daughters, neighbors, and friends.

I confess that what makes my heart jump for joy is when one of these moms tells the truth. When a mom says to me more than "Fine, fine, good, good." Because, thank the good Lord who brought us through, we can finally take off our masks. I honestly don't know if this makes me an upper or a downer, but I come alive when broken pieces are held in the holy place of honest exchange. Like yesterday at my son's basketball game, when a mom told me she was "hanging on by a thread." That the struggles of parenting are wrecking marriages, ruining resolve, and giving the enemy a foothold. Because that's the world. And it's a raw reminder that the din of do-it-all pandemonium is effectively tuning out the "still small voice" (1 Kings 19:11–13, NKJV) of God.

God also made me to love quiet. But, like you, I live here in today's world. Which, like it or not, is not often serene. It is, in fact, working so hard at judging, pressuring, and pushing moms to be more than anyone could possibly be that we are held back from our calling by shame. We look at our outer appearance and overlook our hearts.

If this is not speaking to you, I get that, and I honor that. But my truth is that parenting kids into college has put such a strain on my gentle dream of what motherhood would be like that it sometimes crashes around like a nightmare.

Still, if you gave me a box or a ladder to climb up onto and shout what my heart continues to say, regardless of the world's shoving, it would be this:

You matter. I know it's not about you, or God wouldn't have given you children, but you are such a miracle. You were crafted by a Maker who loves you beyond your wildest dreams. Just the way you are. If you want to change anything about your parenting trajectory, give it to God. Seek peace so you can find His voice over your life. Find joy in how He made you. You are essential. You are enough. Most of all, please don't kill yourself being a false idol. Find out who you really are; and be brave enough to live it out. Your kids will learn great things from you, the greatest of which will be to listen for God's quiet leading over their own lives.

I also hope you love a love story. Because in this book, we'll lean in to the best one ever written as I reach out to you. Throughout this book, we'll pray together, unfold Scripture together, look at what the Bible says together. God is speaking to you. I want His voice to be the One you most desire. So many voices tell moms that we can have it all, do it all, fix it all, and be it all. And they're lying.

If I have it all, I don't need anything, especially God. If I do it all, I don't need anyone else. If I can fix it all, I don't need a Savior. If I think I can be it all, I'm delusional.

Yet somehow, moms especially feel that we have to figure it all out. How to never age, always be kind, give it all away, make millions, inspire the world, raise remarkable problem-free children, and experience no heartache. I have to say it because it's true. We really do believe it's out there. And the tragedy is that we feel we will have no peace until we discover the latest, greatest secret to success.

Meanwhile, we're denying ourselves the simple pleasures of being a mom. We've forgotten that we are children of God.

I'm praying that this book is not just my own personal pep talk. I hope that some moms are feeling me here. I want to be a living experiment in how to listen for God. That's why the first half of this book is literally me walking right into and through the four myths of supermom mania. I will dismantle them with you in real time as I go.

I want to demonstrate that you can do it, too. You can pray for wisdom from the One who made you as a supernatural pathway to living more peacefully. You can transform the lies you may be holding on to or operating under into your own livable truths.

Together, we'll dig into the four myths that moms can have it all, do it all, be it all, and fix it all. We'll look at how we might reframe these for ourselves.

The second half of the book offers quick-read, easy suggestions for walking forward in our newly reframed perspective. We'll try on ideas that cultivate peace. Some may stick; some may require lots of practice; some may inspire your own new ideas.

Every chapter includes open-ended discussion questions for you and God or for you with a group of moms. I hope you will get with your Maker and make a new way forward or gather with others to share your answers.

The second half's desire is to encourage you to listen for and develop your own unique ways of slowing down and accepting God's unshakable love for you.

I'm absolutely certain that God had a specific, mysterious purpose in making each one of us the way He did. I want moms not only to rejoice in their own unique purpose, but also to seek restoration over exhaustion. To pursue silence over stress. To unpack and embrace what Jesus told us in John 16:33 NIV, we will, indeed, have trouble in this world. But what sustains us is His great gift of peace.

You don't have to be a supermom. There's no such thing. But believe me, what God has made you to be is worthy beyond measure.

Lead on, Lord.

part one

digging deep:
the prayerful process
of transforming lies
into truths

1

myth number one: **i can have it all**

*The secret to having it all is
believing you already do.*

—unknown

How did this happen? I look around and see that I'm running after so many unlikely sources of affirmation, only to find that not once has a well-balanced, thoughtfully prepared lunch stood up and said, "Wow! You did all this?" Not once has my vacuum cleaner given me profound insight into my purpose. Even my gray roots mock me—as good as I am about pursuing a head of hair like everyone else's.

All this—homework help, wound-tending, advice-giving, leading, studying, visiting, serving, scheduling, working, cooking, researching, cleaning—has led me no closer to perfection. Only into a new set of idiosyncrasies. As a matter of fact, the only thing it has embroidered into the fabric of my soul is the knowledge that at all times, no matter what the current mix, something's gotta give. Always. Because perfection is a lie without God's grace to fill in the gaps.

Yet I still hear the voices everywhere I go. I see the experts, celebrities, purveyors of fine goods. They all agree: women can have it all. Including everything God gave men. And vice versa. God help us. You see, according to consumerism-pushers, I just need one more thing. Again and again. But who says it should even be mine?

So, let me see. Step one in my experimental walk of shame and renewal—is it the *have*, the *it*, or the *all* that I'm clinging to?

My prayer is this:

Dear God, I have been dancing to a song that may not be the tune You wrote for me. Help me to dissect this heavy myth, word for word. Show me if the pressure I feel to measure up is in the have, *the* it, *or the* all. *Help me hear Your next step for me. Yours, not mine. You made me to follow Your light. You tenderly planted a spark of it in my soul that connects us. Your Word says I am enough. How can I walk away from the worrisome wanting to have it all? To see instead that all I actually need is nothing other than faith? In Jesus' name, Amen.*

I've always been sort of a hippie by nature, preferring to gaze out an open window than into a television or handheld device. I prefer to put my feet in a field of wild clover than in a pedicure chair. Yet as I do what comes naturally to me, I'm inevitably plagued by directives in my head of someone's — anyone's—disapproval. Which actually means I'm allowing others to ridicule what God chooses to do in me. This is the slow practice of silencing my soul's story. And the truth is we each are a critical part of an epic story.

> *Allowing others to ridicule what God chooses to do in me is the slow practice of silencing my soul's story.*

What's more, I still live in the world, just with a heart to not conform to its baser values or temptations. I say this as I recall stuffing cold pizza in my cakehole just hours prior to philosophizing here. Not only charmed by what I know causes a cascade of ill health reactions but giving in happily while walking around doing too many other things simultaneously.

On the one hand, logic assures me that there is no perfection in any mortal. Then why the continual demand to attain it? Not just today, but always? The enchantment of bettering myself does pull me out of pits of frustration, but it can also lead me right into another.

For this time of debunking the I-can-have-it-all myth, I have asked for insight from the one source of true wisdom. Which means I can get my answers in my head, out of the mouths of strangers, in conversation with family and friends…anywhere I choose to trust that the answer is good. And you can, too.

So as I strolled through the grocery store observing the diversity of human desires yesterday, I noticed quite plainly that my *all* is not your *all*. And quite truly, your *all* is not mine. Every cart was unique by design, as were all of us hopefuls who were pushing them around.

I find it enlightening that Colossians 3 explains that Christ is all and is in all. So when seduction takes me slyly by the hand, urging me to have it all, shouldn't I ask if any of it is true, noble, right, pure, lovely, admirable, excellent, or praiseworthy? (Philippians 4:8 NIV). And in so doing, over time, I may come to greater awareness of what *all* means. I imagine my *all* and your *all*, being as different as our grocery lists, have only one thing in common: a satisfying fullness. And here's the paradox. It can come either from receiving or from giving. Each person's path to fullness is unique.

Just as I was writing this, I received a call from a dear friend who shared with me that she was saying yes to too many things at work and feeling like it was pulling her from her family. Sound familiar? Or do you relate to the mom who just can't spread another PB&J today and is in desperate need of adult discussion and grown-up passion?

It reminded me of one of my recent interviews for this book. In response to one of my insecure probes on life, this mom I admire replied, "Well, I know this to be true for me." And she continued by detailing her choice on the matter.

The gift was that as I continued, she stopped me. And she emphasized, "No, really, Lia. Did you hear what I just said? I know this to be true *...for me*. That wisdom has saved me on more occasions than I can count."

Thank you, God, for showing your heart

through other moms. When I'm, in fact, not listening well for God's voice, yet I am asking my soul-deep questions, He can use a friend to make me listen. God can use another mom who knows the struggle to show me how to trust the insight He supplies. My friend owning what works *for her* really worked for her. Which gives me courage. Because of her clarity, I can also know that when I'm seeking divine guidance, I can trust what seems to work for me and my children. Even if other moms do it differently. Because we should be able to try what works for us.

On the other hand, even when God's voice gets through to me, I still have a tendency to doubt. This is one of my quirks that my kids like to encourage me to quit. Here's the dilemma, which maybe you've also felt: How many times has God come through for me, and I still dare to not believe and trust? I still stand on the edge of the proverbial pool, and I don't jump in.

This is why the transcendent practice of *eucharisteo* celebrated in Ann Voskamp's delicious book *One Thousand Gifts* is such an eye-opener. This escapade is Voskamp's urging to be grateful for all of it. If we zoom in on this tiny word *all*, we see that, in truth, it includes good, bad, boring, heartbreaking, tiring, annoying, thrilling—the works. And we don't have to master it all because God is always at work. We are not humanly capable of making it all turn out perfect. Says Voskamp, when we stop treating life like an emergency or an impending disaster and start treating it like a gift to be noticed slowly, we learn to count on God for all of it. To actually give thanks in times of worry, fear, or suffering because God is good and so sovereign that we are delivered into His greater plan regardless. The same way Jesus gave thanks while breaking bread that signified his imminent crucifixion.

I've also recently discovered, thanks to Kaia Roman's empowering book *The Joy Plan*, that thinking positively can actually rewire our brains. Permanently. In a new direction. Which scientifically attracts the positive things we imagine. So when we are inclined to think ourselves lacking if we don't have it all, we can change our mindset. In the book, Roman explains a mindfulness exercise she teaches with a single sheet of paper. She asks participants to fold their paper in half and crease it well. They then fold and crease it again. Then she asks them to unfold their paper and refold it.

What they witness is how effortlessly the paper folds itself the next time along creases they purposely created. It's a visual aid to demonstrate that what we say in our heads becomes our well-worn thought-roads. We get comfortable there. We fold easily, even into lies. We can put ourselves on the slippery fast track to depression. But truly, because of our God-given miraculous brain, we can also think new thoughts and go a totally different direction. We can reroute our potential with what we believe in our heads. We can, as I heard it coined by a local pastor, "live differently."

So instead of riding the speedway of have-it-all aggression, maybe I should make a new fold. I can tell myself that life and all that is in it never "belongs" to me or to any one of us.

None of us are the "haves."

We are all the borrowers. Borrowers of moments we can attempt to honor into memories that sweeten with the passing of time. Life is owned, balanced, nurtured, and nourished by God. So what do I have but that which is passing through my hands? And I have my answer.

I cannot have it all. But I believe that I can always have all I need.

Which raises some questions: Is having it all, in fact, a myth? A losing proposal? Or is it truth, just in an entirely different light than today's rush of fear, greed, and i-everything has cast it?

If God alone has it all, what has He given me as part of that all? Because God has it all, I thank Him that it is not under my feeble dominion.

I intend to start noticing and celebrating my own proverbial grocery cart or basket of all. This way, I'll know what's in it, and what's not. For now. I'll see how I'm different in capacity, ability, even willingness from anyone else—by God's design.

Starting now, I commit to establishing an active, present-tense account of realizations like these: Today I don't have _____, but I do have _____. Right now, I can't have _____, but I can have _____. Even now, I may not have certainty on this myth's impact on my sense of peace (and I may never have it), but I do have a desire to search through it and learn what it means to me.

To boot, Romans 3:23 assures me that all fall short, no matter how much each one has. Including health, wealth, smarts, talent, stuff, and more. So if I choose to hold out my hands not in self-focused desperation but in gratitude and humility, I suspect I will more readily discard trying to have it all. Then I can replace it with living gladly with all God has given already and continues to give anew.

Allow me a raw caveat here. I've just finished

exchanging the day's news with my delightful teenage daughter. As part of it, she read aloud to me an excerpt from her personal journal, which she had also read aloud in her creative writing class. It was angry, bitter, and toxic.

All this, after my having poured my love and attention into her, preparing her with esteem in abundance. Or so I, pretentiously, assumed.

After honest words between us, we came to the agreement that all people, regardless of their situations, experience the emotion of anger. And it was not on me to take responsibility for that appearing in her life. We all struggle with an onslaught of backbiting, gossip, lies, betrayals, pressures, and pains that cause spider cracks in our foundations. Writing through it was her way of recognizing, owning, and calling attention to her need for healthy boundaries as she navigates her way to womanhood.

Let go of having entirely smiley, well-balanced, never-frazzled, harmonious children. Because it just isn't real.

Today, you and I can let go of having entirely smiley, well-balanced, never-frazzled, harmonious children. Because it just isn't real. And not battling with a full range of emotions leaves us with less life. Recently, I

28

melted as I read my daughter's latest entry in our kitchen countertop collection of one thousand gifts that we're noticing and writing down together. She wrote, "Being OK with not always being OK." Her honesty relaxed my grip on life and filled me up with grace to grow.

So, step 2...when the nagging sense returns that I'm in need, missing out, failing, or unfulfilled, I intend to trust God's provision. Did He assign me to hurt myself? Hate myself? Or does God long for me to claim that He has it all and then for me to give it back to Him in faith, allowing Him to amaze me? But how? When money's tight, cuts don't heal, things aren't guaranteed, bills get late, how do I simply trust?

By praying.

I can pray for the courage to unclench and step off the crazy train. Take off my figurative protective gear and switch to what I feel comfortable in. Then I can turn to the leadership of Jesus, back down the road through memories of meeting God in the most tender and reserved of my personal places. Becoming more certain that having it all is thieving falsely from the One who *is* all.

I think the *all* that this popular myth is speaking of, when it's viewed in the light that reveals it to be a myth, is composed of wants.

So how can I illustrate, especially to my own children, that no mom or mom-to-be has it all?

I go back to the basket we are each holding, and over it we can observe, "She may not have _____, but she sure has _____. She won't have _____ for a while, but she will surely have _____," and so on. The beautiful portrait it paints is that together we have all that God envisions. Not any one of us alone.

What's more, like it or not, millionaire, brainiac, model, or supermom, there are things that cannot be controlled or perfected.

Consider the weather. If I ever feel big about any accomplishment, I'm washed with the certainty that tsunamis, hurricanes, earthquakes, avalanches, volcanoes, and any number of weather miracles can instantly call the shots. Obliterating every *have*, *it*, and *all*.

For that matter, any unforeseen human crisis can exact its own obliteration as well. The upturning of our tightly woven containers happens. Allowing them to be refilled is our part.

So, Mom, let's try to find some joy in whatever we currently have in our baskets. God fills them on His timeline, takes from them to redistribute for His purposes, and fills them again to overflowing. He can turn a basket of five loaves and two fish into a banquet for thousands. Let's love and share our temporary "haves" supplied by the One who owns it all. Remember, it is flowing. It is not baggage. We have holding places within, full of changing gifts.

For the rest of this month, I want to deliberately take gracious inventory. I hope you will, too. *Lord, I thank You that I may not have the energy I used to, but I do have more patience now. I thank You that I may not have a glorious wardrobe, but I have jeans that feel like a true friend.*

Try to find joy in whatever's in your basket. God can turn five loaves and two fish into a banquet.

These are just a few of my fulfilling, passing "haves," and I'm positive you have yours, too. As I hold open my basket, I let God surprise me. Which quenches my burning desire to have it all by material or societal standards or in any finite or completed manner.

I simply stand amazed that right now, I have all I need and enough to share with someone in need.

Khalil Gibran said that the deeper sorrow carves into you, the more joy you can contain. So I can imagine that each of us is an ever-complete creation, whether hollow or filled. We are each useful to God for His plan. Which is precisely why, I suppose, that when I give, especially when I give sacrificially and not easily out of my overage, I feel deeply filled.

Hence, it is in giving that having is consummated.

Do I have nothing when I am hungry or when I am overstuffed? Is there ever truly a state in which I need to have all that I presently don't? Or are all my hollows, in fact, receptacles for grace and the gifts that others were created to offer? And am I always, then, completely filled?

The celebrated poet Goethe once wrote, "It is the nature of grace to fill the places that have been empty." This suggests that we aren't even in charge of the action of filling up our have-not areas. It will happen by God.

I believe if we strive instead for presence in each hour given to each of us, rather than racing past them toward having more, we will come closest to the "full life" spoken of in John 10:10. A life in which, in each moment, we are fully being, not impressively doing. If you and I are still here, in this world, even if either of our baskets is full of temporary troubles, we are still needed in this place, in this time, by our Creator. And He will see to it that we make it through.

I think we were given minds to sift through the messages even if they truly are coming at an unprecedented pace now. We can still practice our authentic no. Because a lot of the stuff you're being told you must have, you really don't need. Possibly don't even want. Even if—I'll say it—it's dressed up in faith-based service.

Three words I'd love to hear less: *Must. Have. More.* Tuck this away: if you don't buy or do that today, you can still talk to your God about it tomorrow. You won't miss out on that.

This feels like my step 3 here. Today is the day to reword this I-can-have-it-all myth. Because it points to the truth:

Today, I have all I need, thanks to the grace of God.

for individual reflection
or group discussion

1. In what ways does the world prey on your sense of lack or need?

2. What needs does God supply for you in your parenting and marriage?

3. How have times of loss and uncertainty brought you to a new sense of contentment?

4. How does it feel to you when you hear an ad proclaiming, "You can have it all"?

5. Do you really want it all?

6. Does knowing (or being told) that you can have it all create a sense of incompleteness in you?

7. What can you accept not having, now that you are a mom?

8. Do you know a mom who admits her areas of need happily? How does that inspire you?

2

myth number two: **i can do it all**

Martha, Martha...you are worried and upset about many things, but only one thing is needed. Mary has chosen what is better and it will not be taken away from her.

—Luke 10:41–42 (NIV)

I'm fairly confident that if you're still with me, you have a true-life story or two (or more) about a time when you realized you couldn't do all things. For me it was as I began investing my interest, attention, and love in the children God gave to me and my husband.

I used to slam dunk most tests I studied for. I'd land nearly every job I interviewed for. I paid my bills on time. I earned clients' long-term respect. I could clean my apartment all night and shine at work the next day.

Enter marriage and kids. With their lifelong accomplice, aging.

Slowly, the varnish fades, the covering cracks, the mess I am becoming and have always been oozes out all over the floor. And sometimes, I can't sweep it up for days. When I simply couldn't think of another craft and I napped right next to my toddler, guilty of leaving both the dishes and the yard work undone. When I can't think of how to reenergize my kids after they've had a long, hard school day and I overdo it on brownies with them instead, my imaginary cookie continues to crumble. When I yell at my husband when talking would suffice, I face my frailty.

And as my youngsters are growing into a preteen athlete and a teenage scholar and environmentalist, not only do my intentions fail me, my actual body's ability does, too. Now my résumé wilts with accomplishments such as "stayed up longer than I thought was physically possible, to fit in some quality time with my son or daughter."

Sometimes, seeking God's truth can be more confusing than clarifying. Because Philippians 4:13 says I can do all things. But don't miss that the credit here is given to Christ. Without the strength He supplies, I can do nothing good. What's more, I wonder if what we heap on our to-do lists are really things we feel the world commanding, not God. Help me with this, God.

So my ordinary prayer as I unwind from the I-can-do-it-all myth is this:

Heavenly Father, You created me. You know why I do the things I do. You know about the sleepy streak You wove into me. You created my craving for fresh air, my distaste for stress, my love of stand-up comedy. You see me make my to-do lists and criticize myself when I can't do them all. I misunderstand how much "doing" is enough. Show me how to position my heart. Give me words to repeat like a song that will ease my shame of not doing all the things it looks like others are doing. Help me accept each day's bouquet as a romantic connection between You and me. An arrangement of originality gathered from the things You empowered me to manage today. Help me be thankful that I am able at all, rather than desirous of greater ability. Show me how to rewrite the do-it-all myth. Help me to choose the things You would have me do. In Jesus' name, Amen.

If you ever get the notion that your neck or

back is stiffening from a load you're not carrying well, I recommend grabbing a pen (or whatever techno-device you text with, video with, or speak into to record things). There's something curiously therapeutic about pouring your prayer out through your hand, mouth, or mind. A good honest love letter is never wasted. My encouragement to you is simply that when you pray, I promise, love is streaming.

So, after emptying myself through prayer, my first reaction to probing Philippians 4:13 is that God does not want you to carry His load. He doesn't need you to. He does call, invite, and even command us to participate but never to take over being God.

I believe "all things" (or in other translations "all this" or "everything") that the Word speaks of is specifically my unique *all* in this moment and yours, too. For this, I am refusing to research commentaries on what this passage means because this book's central goal is to boost your trust in the Creator to speak wisdom specifically written for you alone into your very private panic, pain, or passion. No one, absolutely no one, knows you like God does. So my resolve as I

No one, absolutely no one, knows you like God does.

follow this idea right now is to lay down my pen and wait. To open a window of time to receive His wisdom for me. Lord, hear my prayer.

This is just how cool God is.

As I sat utterly silent, waiting, His tenderness eventually appeared. He whispered within me, "You may not want to look up commentaries, but I want you to know more. I want you to pick up your Bible. Read around the passage with me."

Now at this point you may be thinking, "OK, lady's lost it. She hears voices?" In response, I challenge: If you are utterly silent for as long as it takes, yet you are inwardly open and asking… don't you? Not an audible, clear sentence, but an intuition. An urging. An *inspiration*. Which, dissected, means "to breathe in." As you breathe, something invisible and inaudible most certainly fills you, supplying a basic need. You don't just apply inspiration like a stick-on externally. You inhale it into yourself. It moves you silently from within.

So, as I follow inspiration to read the words building up to Philippians 4:13, I notice that Paul first states that he is not "in need." He has learned to be content in any circumstance. He has been in need and had plenty. But the secret to not needing to have it all or do it all, I hear in his words as he continues, is that his strength at all times comes from Christ. Christ's spirit within him. And you. And me. At the end of Philippians 4, Paul says, "To our God and Father be the glory for ever and ever."

I think a large part of shedding the burden of doing it all is realizing you're not alone. Never is it all up to you. The world is not being balanced on anyone's index finger. If you or I ever truly had to do it all, what would be God's purpose for creating everyone else? In making babies? In orchestrating the seasons? Are any of us authors of these?

Shedding the burden of doing it all begins with realizing you're not alone. Never is it all up to you.

But we are given the will to choose.

Just the other day, a girlfriend of mine was sharing that her volunteering load felt heavy. Granted, she was doing more than I am currently, or so it seemed to me, but her heart was moved by a blog post she'd read that explained, "Every time you say yes to something, you say no to something else." For her, in this season, it felt as though her busyness was an outright no to time she desired with her kids. To be fair, every mom has her own yes-no formula. For some, it may be that saying yes to another afternoon of quality time for the kids' sake means saying no to self-care that would do more good. My ultimate hope here is a heightened propensity to listen more intently to God's directions for *you*. Followed by the courage to choose.

Which illustrates this phenomenon: we all have twenty-four hours in a day. We all fill them up. We all "do." The "doing it all" seems to be in comparison to what others are doing. Because we are all doing.

It's a fact: being is actually essential to our doing. Otherwise, God would not have invented sleep. Nor would the Creator Himself have taken Sabbath. But He did. God's biorhythm for us does include rest. He invites you to rest in Matthew 11:28: "Come to me, all you who are weary and burdened, and I will give you rest."

This philosophy of being is fabulously rolled out in Dr. David Kundtz's book *Stopping: How to Be Still When You Have to Keep Going*. While manifesting a concept he terms "stopovers," Kundtz explains, "If being loving to yourself is not good enough reason for you, consider this: A stopover is an act of generosity for others in your life and the world at large. A composed and focused soul is a deep richness for all the world, a great gift for those who encounter you, and

41

a desperately needed example in this off-kilter world." (Kundtz, 1998)

Put like that, it's reason enough for me to at least stop and ask myself what things I'm doing that are wearing me out. Space, attention, relaxation, openness, and solitude are gifts worth giving. To yourself or anyone else. They are where you can experience God.

Never would the One who made you say, "Don't rest; that's bad." He wouldn't nag, "You should feel guilty for recharging your energy in the way I created you to."

No, that voice is the enemy.

And this race to do it all? It's a battle we ought not to be fighting. Rather than rage against ourselves, we ought to fight off the self-punitive destruction wrought by the father of lies. Dare I say, our coconspirator in the creation of oppressive myths?

Why do I guilt myself over expectations that are not God's for me? In comparison (sneaky word), I am not doing as much as other moms I see. Celebrities, for example. Single moms who hold full-time jobs. Missionaries. Teachers. Nurses. My list goes on. But in preparing, listening, and offering this small book, my intent is to quiet the mania of doing more than is needed. Or doing to my destruction. Or, best of all, to do away with doing more solely to compete and compare. As a replacement, I can hang on to the assertion that God gave me the freedom to continuously choose yes or no. As a mania override, I would rather ask God to show me his uses for me, then step into my day, trusting that He will.

You and I were created for divine, supernatural, mysterious reasons. Today, one reason may be to nourish my family. Next week, it may be to research how to become a foster parent. Another day, it may be to repair the bike my son rides to school on warm days. If I was doing it all, I couldn't do the one thing well that the Holy Spirit is leading me toward.

As a mania override, ask God to show you his uses for you, today. Then step into the day trusting that He will.

Doing what's best may be pushing past a fear, accepting an award, building a well, showing someone the world, or holding someone's hand as he or she crosses into Heaven. The thing is, we are not in control of why He is doing what He does through willing hearts. The only skin we have in the game is exercising our yes and no. Then, to trust that if we falter or fail or break, God can do something better with it.

Going forward, I want my doing to feel more like a trusting obedience than an exhaustive race toward acknowledgment or social media status. After all, who am I trying to impress?

If I give an open heart to God and know that He created my simplicity masterfully, I have nothing to prove. Even better, nothing to fear. Which doesn't mean I won't *feel* fear, but I can focus my energy on asking if God is leading me to take this on or if it is instead pride, anger, greed, or any other power that is creating my controlling desire for any fearful choice.

Of course, I'm not saying that I simply do whatever I want. Or sit around and wait for God to push me. Scripture warns against succumbing to our fleshly desires. God knows our tendencies and is fully aware that we are often trapped. But if I give each simple choice I make leading to each action I take, every yes or no, to God for His use, then I can hope He will continue to impart wisdom for the way. I've never forgotten the simplest prayer: "Use me." All that says is, "I am not the Maker, but what You made here is wide open to Your purposes."

To feel in close connection with God's spirit, I highly recommend reading the New Testament. So much is in it about how Jesus sees things, feels things, cares for things—all things. My highest goal, rather than attempting to be Jesus, would be to do my few small things the way He would.

In other words, if I know God's will is always purer than my own, then I trust that what little I'm able to accomplish can be perfected by Him—not me. I'm hoping that, although I will still make lists, goals, deadlines, appointments, and plans—as well as mistakes—I will see doing it all as God's collective work, not mine alone. And reaching back into Philippians 4, let's embrace that even the glory—especially the glory—for all this doing goes to God.

Embrace that the glory for all our doing belongs to God.

Case in point: I'm prone to fancy myself a good mom. I aim to uplift, enjoy, and guide my kids. However, somehow, I have participated in fostering somewhat of a class cutup, who has been described to me by some of his teachers as a "disruption."

I am learning, by grace, to like this word *disrupt.*

Because as God, through my son, shines light on my pride and oversight, I am pulled to my knees. In need of ability higher than my own.

Unable to take credit for anything. Humility hurts. But I am discovering it is a good pain. Too much of me is imbalance. And too much expectation of others to justify me is too much pressure on the family.

So, I ask for God's words, I form them to my son, and I likely still miss the mark. The real deal is that everything we say to each of our children is a first-time experiment with that child. That child you're speaking to is a masterpiece with a future you cannot foresee. No matter how much parenting you've done. My son is a dear, creative, kindhearted, comedy-loving, athletic, distracted, wildly intelligent fifteen-year-old boy. And although I can impart my been-there-done-that, let's-get-prepared-for-real-life speeches, I am no better than he. He is a glorious work in progress in God's hands. As am I. And you. And all your children, too. I can't do my son's life. You can't do your children's lives. And vice versa.

The real deal is that everything we say to each of our children is a first-time experiment. Each child has a future you cannot foresee.

Having established that, I still believe we benefit from reading good books, welcoming advice from friends and loved ones, listening to sermons, and receiving helpful messages. We can also ask God to show us the poor, oppressed, widowed, and orphaned He intends for us to assist. My experience has been, though, that we are not the best measurers of who is in need in our circle of influence.

Without consulting our Creator, we may operate on wants and substitute them as fulfillment. We wind up chasing tax-deductible, public, proven, visible, recorded donations. However, the most spiritually malnourished souls in need of my presence may be myself, my husband, my neighbor, or one of my kids or their friends. It's possible that your largest donation to date may be the sweet, simple act of putting your arm around the person next to you. You may not even have to contribute to his or her bottom line or drop off items. Having little stuff does not automatically indicate having little. Throwing stuff at a problem is not always the cure. Genuine needs can be difficult to fathom. To boot, your response to God's leading may feel completely anonymous. But let me assure you, God sees. Believe me, to the Maker of eternity, even the smallest gestures offered in faith are enough.

As we are washed in a life of continual needs, my hope is just that moms can feel invited to let it all rain over and around us like a refreshing pool of possibilities without the insanity of saying yes to doing it all. Our differences in ability make His world a more balanced and colorful place. I believe we can find our own answers in peace and quiet more clearly than in the din of do-it-all pandemonium.

Owning that not one of us can do it all means we're practicing compassion on ourselves so we can extend it to others. It means we always have someone to care with, care for, admire, and join along the way. We cannot escape that we all are laden with imperfection. Sin, selfishness, judgment, and a host of human traits plague us daily. Hourly. Any second now. What's more, circumstances throw us off course. The unexpected can rewrite our choices instantly. Not one of us will walk through all times exactly like Jesus. But we are all given opportunities to try. And the invitation to rest and recharge.

> *Owning that not one of us can do it all means we're practicing compassion on ourselves so we can extend it to others.*

Now my I-can-do-it-all rewritten myth reads like this:

I can do what I choose to do in this moment, God leading and willing.

for individual reflection
or group discussion

1. How has an apparent failure helped improve you?

2. Have you ever tried to do it all? What did it teach you?

3. What are one or two to-dos on your do-it-all list that you could let go?

4. How could you say no to something and, in doing so, say yes to something better?

5. What is your system for laying out your to-dos? What do you give yourself grace on?

6. How did you feel the last time you chose to step through one open door option and forgo others?

7. Is it possible that you are trying to do so many things that you are only expending a small amount of energy and effect in several areas?

8. In what area would you like to concentrate your efforts?

9. Above all, what do you believe God has made you to do?

3

myth number three: **i can be it all**

"But what about you?" he asked.
"Who do you say I am?"

—Matthew 16:15 (NIV)

If you can't be you, who will? If I can't stay curious about what feels constructive and right or good to me, how can anyone really help or know me? How can I expect to make a positive impact with my life if I don't listen to the wisdom that runs within my soul?

Within me is a way of processing; within you

is yours. I'm like the baking soda to your flour. The dirt to your sunshine. However you like to visualize it, without your kind of mothering, I am not fully my own kind of mom. I stand in odd complement to all that you are. Spreading this out a bit further, we begin to glimpse the profound: our children come directly through us or grow up within our direction but will never be exactly like us. They grow into larger someones we are not meant to fully identify with or completely understand. Same goes for our husbands, and so on. So why do we punish ourselves trying to be something other than what God gives us to work with? Why do I see a world of roles for moms and think myself defective until I've fulfilled them all?

I suppose an ingredient in this glitchiness is our human habit of hope. Hope is our daily revival, our continual lifeline, our long-range vision. Without hope, we shrivel. But why hope to be a different mom? Why strive to be a mom achieving things that are, in truth, not my heart's desire? I do encourage becoming a better version of myself—as in more patient, less snappy, a gradual improvement. But why be someone *not* myself?

Living is wasted on lies fabricated while simply wishing. I wish I had _____ hair. I wish I had _____ legs. I wish I had her way of _____.

I wish I had her knack for _____. Unless God gave it to me, my desire to be it all is one part coveting and the other part pride.

The truth tells me clearly that God, the Maker of Heaven and Earth, was before all and made all and is all (Psalm 146:6 NIV, Colossians 1:17 NIV). You and I are but a sparkle in an infinite sea of glittering profound potential. Being all roles, things, or sources to anyone or any group is a God-size goal. And thank God, you and I are not that size. Unfortunately, there is a vast range of maniacal routes we can wander in the contest to be it all. External, internal, geographical.

Being all roles, things, or sources to anyone or any group is a God-size goal. And thank God, you and I are not that size.

If I strive to be her or them—here, there, and everywhere—I disintegrate. There simply isn't all the stuff God's made of in me alone. I am, however, a necessary facet of His reflection. As are you. I may figuratively be his hands or feet, but I may also serve as the eye, ear, toe, elbow, or shoulder. We are each a part of a total being of humanity, not everything to everyone. It's just not wise. Or possible. Or God's design.

In exploring this myth, I sense a quest

not only for rewriting it, but also for a new declaration. Because I believe Jesus, one of the finest life coaches, laid an example of the power of saying so. When discussing His own identity, Jesus asks Peter, "Who do you say I am?" It mattered to God to urge Peter to say who God was, separate from who Peter was. To see if truth would be proclaimed. In this story, even today, we are challenged to declare what is true. And one reality is that if you are here, the world needs you. The way you are.

My effect on the world around me, like it or not, begins with how I interact with myself. My reality begins with how I identify myself. Who I say I am.

Can I live with myself? What am I capable of bettering within myself? What am I not capable of doing? What talent is God developing in me? How am I unique? What am I here for? These are questions that naturally bubble up from my center and yours as well. As I prepare to lay myself open to God's work with this nonsensical myth of being it all, here is my prayer:

Dear God, I want to know why I ever thought, or will ever think, that I could be it all. Mother, friend, helper, fixer, cook, teacher, lover, organizer, volunteer, caterer, entertainer, fundraiser, driver, mentor, maker…even, God forbid, savior. What is this unending list of "What do I want to be?" that haunts and drives moms like me? As I long to be someone else, I prop up yet another impostor, rather than who You made me to be. I am clouded. Pressed. Multitasking beyond my capacity. As I open my eyes and heart to Your signs and leading, show me how to be content with simply being, rather than being it all. To be what You would have me be, instead of all-inclusive. Show me how to be an original package, not the total package. Erase deceptions, God, and guide me back to peace. In Jesus' name, Amen.

Yesterday at church, our pastor brought up the famous first line of Rick Warren's best-selling book *The Purpose-Driven Life*. Warren begins this extraordinary exposé on discovering meaning in your existence with the no-apologies opener: "It's not about you."

Respectfully, because I appreciate Rick Warren, his insights, and that book, I still desire to add, "But you matter very much." Like all of us, Rick Warren has had his share of unthinkable calamity, and I still believe with him in the call to put others' needs ahead of our own as a practice for spiritual growth. I think where it can get misleading is when we overstep the existence of ourselves as a valuable vessel through which service is supplied. I fear that, in society's quickness to assume that being Christian is all about impossible sacrifice or earning angel points based on who sees us giving (no matter how it compromises our sanity), we can weaken the simple tool God made each of us to be.

Don't overstep your existence as a valuable vessel through which service is supplied. Striving for impossible sacrifice can weaken that vessel.

If we look very closely at Philippians 2:1–4 (ESV), which in some versions is subtitled "Christ's Example of Humility," He says, "Complete my joy by being of the same mind, having the same love, being in full accord and of one mind. Do nothing from selfish ambition or conceit, but in humility count others more significant than yourselves. Let each of you look not only to his own interests, but also to the interests of others."

There are more examples of truths in the Word that hearten us to consider others, but I want to venture a guess that a great majority of moms can do this to a self-damaging degree. Christ is saying here, very clearly, look not only to your own interests, but after doing so and finding yourself in a position of willingness and honest humility, count others more significant...after you have reckoned with yourself and addressed your needs rather than your wants. This is because you realize that the purpose of Christ's power within you is so that its abundance can flow out to others whose lives you touch.

Savor those two potent little words in Philippians 2:1–4 (ESV): *not only*. The other idea here is that depletion can also occur if we only focus on self. Not that we shouldn't nurture ourselves, but that shouldn't be all we look at all the time. It's likely because focusing inward for too long can block the flow of energy and love outward that God desires to accomplish through you.

Look to your needs. Tend to them. For the significant purpose of serving others.

Yet I feel a hesitance to overextend willy-nilly in service to burnout. This others-focused life we moms are leading can get clogged up with way too many requests, too many voices, too many activities. And it's enticing, every day. We want to chase away the guilt that comes from wanting to be everything to everyone we love or meet—at a dear price.

As I pondered this problem, I pored through the New Year's "Let It Go" issue of *Real Simple* magazine and lit upon a mighty message from author Brigid Schulte:

> For women, guilt is poisonous. We feel guilty if we're overachieving. We feel guilty if the house is dirty. At-home moms feel guilty

about not contributing financially; working moms, about not spending enough time with their kids. But let's take a breath and realize we have impossible ideals. I do more stuff with my kids than my mom did. She used to lock us out of the house when she was out shopping, and we would break the basement window to get in. If I did something like that, child protective services would get called. You feel less guilty if you decide that every day you're going to do the best you can. Recognize that what you do is good enough. (Schulte, 2015)

As this repeats in my head, I pray it will lodge in my heart: decide every day to do the best I can and recognize that it is good enough. Otherwise, the numbing and paralyzing effects of self-hatred have their hold.

I'd like to point out here that a daily resolution to do my best cultivates my will. And interestingly, exercising my will blossoms into willingness. Simply being willing to do your day with a heart given to God's greater plan and His endless ability and love for us isn't a weak position. In fact, grasping tightly and demanding more or spewing dissatisfaction only weakens your soul's power.

Remember, a soul at peace, willing to not

be everything to everyone but grateful to be enough, is a gift.

Since when are guilt, remorse, regret, complaints, or disappointment good gifts to give? I realize they can be gifts of maturity when we walk through them ourselves, but they are not where God would have us remain. They are often instead, symptoms of this hurried, judgmental world for which all of us are responsible, but they are not fruits of the Spirit at peace.

Let's remind ourselves that if we are daily inviting and breathing to life the Holy Spirit within each of us, we are equipped to manifest the fruits of love, joy, peace, patience, kindness, goodness, faithfulness, gentleness, and self-control (Galatians 5:22–23). Admittedly, I rarely if ever will be all these on any given day. But I can wake up willing to practice in the way God made me to be.

Remember, a soul at peace, willing to not be everything to everyone but grateful to be enough, is a gift.

You see, when I am content to be me—instead of trying to be everything to everyone—I have greater flexibility to be happy to see you, be with you, share in the body. It is God's design that we complement each other's intentional areas of emptiness or need. Romans 12:4–8 NIV explains:

> For just as each of us has one body with many members, and these members do not all have the same function, so in Christ we, though many, form one body, and each member belongs to all the others. We have different gifts, according to the grace given to each of us. If your gift is prophesying, then prophesy in accordance with your faith; if it is serving, then serve; if it is teaching, then teach; if it is to encourage, then give encouragement; if it is giving, then give generously; if it is to lead, do it diligently; if it is to show mercy, do it cheerfully.

Ephesians 4:16 (NLT) further clarifies: "He makes the whole body fit together perfectly. As each part does its own special work, it helps the other parts grow, so that the whole body is healthy and growing and full of love."

Bringing that home to our modern human experience, Mother Theresa offers, "If we have no peace, it is because we have forgotten that we belong to each other."

This is why any human with a heart is touched when athletes of any capacity, for example, go back and help a fallen fellow runner, rather than frantically speeding to victory over their peers. This heart position does not negate the famous Hebrews 12 verse that encourages us to "run with perseverance the race marked out for us, fixing our eyes on Jesus." It, in fact, illustrates that the race marked out for us, as we focus on Jesus, may involve unexpected turnarounds and detours. Regardless of our lane position at any one time, we are intrinsically aware that we are all in this together. Somehow, as we race to and through adulthood, we can lose sight of this innocence. Acknowledging it, as we witness unguarded demonstrations of love, pierces us, allowing a river of mercy. And the really great news is that in that river, there is a soul-quenching hydration that refuels us for life and sustains without depletion. This concept is confirmed in John 7:38 when Jesus says, "Whoever believes in me, as Scripture has said, rivers of living water will flow from within them."

While flailing my pen to record these thoughts, I had seconds prior been boring myself to a vacuous depth on my home elliptical. Methodically cycling, thirsty for strength, I grabbed a nearby notebook and was filled with living water. That moment I allowed what God was saying to me to flow out on paper was the instant that time disappeared. I ceased to be aware of its boundaries. I let God's voice have life through my hand, and I let go of any constraint, self-doubt, body image, or goal. I dove right into a state of openness. It provided me the image of runners who carry each other forward, and I allowed it to be good enough. Time collapsed, and in what seemed like a mere few breaths, my thirty-minute timer beeped. I had no idea I was even close to being done working out.

Some call this state of being a "flow" state. What is yours? It can give you a good sense of who God made you to be. It can change depending on your life's circumstances. In this current season, I now know my daughter's flow state. Only because she thrilled me one day by describing an essay she was asked to write about her own personal state of flow: the essence of existence when time diminishes and life rushes in at full buoyancy. Flow is when you are carried by the joy of the moment, content to be exactly as you are.

Discover your flow state: the essence of existence when time diminishes and you are content to be exactly as you are.

Even as well as I thought I knew my own daughter, I guessed her flow state incorrectly multiple times. Instead, her answer punctured me. Although she came from the womb of a broken, semi-introverted scaredy-cat like me, the flow state of the young woman standing before me was none other than *delivering a monologue on stage.* Whoa. Now I know for sure that I did not do that. God made that. That kind of mysterious anomaly to myself is none other than the handiwork of her Creator. He made her to be most herself in a place where I would instantly break out in a sweat. So it goes: I cannot be her, or you, or anyone else but me, and for good reason.

Here are some others I cannot be. I need their strengths to get through this life. I need authors who rock my world so I can reopen the eyes of my heart. A yoga teacher whose flow is balancing so I can try to stretch myself. I need a farmer who cares passionately about nutrition so I can learn how the body responds to food. I need teachers who are better teachers for my kids on many subjects than I am. Foodies who can teach humanity how to combine flavors that nourish, heal, and delight.

> *Rather than being all, be still. As you are softer and kind to yourself, you are being the essence God created you to be.*

I need so many God-made creations other than myself. I need trees, for goodness' sake, to breathe. Pets to exemplify unconditional love and to test my patience. The list of what I simply cannot be but definitely need is infinite.

Try this at points during your day: rather than being all, be still. As you are softer and are kind to yourself, allowing your breath to deepen, you are being the essence God created you to be. You are allowing God to cease your striving and open your well. A dry well irrigates nothing. So simply being is a necessary component of equipping yourself to be all you can be.

There's a plethora of modern commands to be intentional. My counteroffer is to practice exhaling as well and to be grateful to be enough. To put down our "intentions" remote controls and remain a bit more open to God's direction and timing.

Who are you being right now? Like a flower in a vast garden of species, you create a splash of color that only you know how to offer, instinctively. Receive the acceptance and appreciation that is God's eternal blessing over His workmanship. See Ephesians 2:4-10 NIV. You are a vessel that He is pouring His presence through to those your life touches.

Choose one significant or original thing you know about yourself. Imagine how amazing it is that God enjoys seeing you use that gift. Relax in knowing that it's a much larger work, well beyond our own wits, that masterminds our world. Maybe you'll sense it, too, in this poem offered to me over lunch by my wise and wonderful mom:

> *Little drops of water,*
> *Little grains of sand,*
> *Make the mighty ocean*
> *And the pleasant land.*
> *Thus the little minutes,*
> *Humble though they be,*
> *Make the mighty ages*
> *Of eternity.*

—Julia Abigail Fletcher Carney

Today, I resolve to walk the way that naturally comes to me. To not pretend to agree with everyone's ideas, but rather listen to them. To know that where God guides my feet, He needs me the way I am. Even without makeup, certainly without fear or pretense, completely without judgment or vengeance. I can only be who I am being in the moment. And try only to be true with grace and kindness. As I am responding to texts from friends while writing these thoughts, I cannot also be the other things I had planned: family dog-walker, house-cleaner, or career-seeker. Right now, I am a mother and a friend. And I am hearing a whisper to reword the I-can-be-it-all myth into what is true:

Simply being who I am contributes to God's plan.

for individual reflection
or group discussion

1. In what ways does the world tempt you to play too many roles at once?

2. Why do you think moms sometimes pretend to be the type of person who feels fabricated or not genuine to herself?

3. In what ways can you be more authentic, without assuming they are or need to be super or superlative?

4. Who do you say that you are?

5. How can you give yourself room to "not be" one of your roles sometimes?

6. Who in your life plays a unique role that you cannot?

7. How do you fill that need for someone else?

8. Do you feel a nagging need to be good at everything?

9. What can you laugh out loud about just not being?

10. Are you ready to let God be all and be just part of His ability?

4

myth number four: **i can fix it all**

*The things in life that bring the most pleasure
always make a mess.*

—Lee Pearson Knapp, author of *Grace in the First Person*

My stomach is swollen from overuse. And not enough tending. What is enough? To feel balanced, semi-calm, and fairly well. My son has the flu today, and I strain to recall the last time he was sick. It's been a relatively mild winter, and word on the street is that half the basketball league is out with the flu. My son's team had only six boys show up to practice the other night, one of whom we now know had the flu. His pediatrician's daughter's team had only five at her last game, she said. Yet here was my family's pediatrician—a strong, smart woman and mom—at work.

Does it ever seem to you that the entire universe is working at generously gainful employment whenever you're home with a sick child? What is this odd, solitary imprisonment from reality? On a larger scale, I sense that work-at-home moms everywhere are struggling more than we ever discuss. With fear of having neither honor nor money. Sure, we talk up the many other rewards and dividends. We feel doubly blessed if we share this lifelong task with employed husbands who love and care. But we know, intrinsically, that our husbands are human, too, and subject to all the what-ifs of our broken, sinful world.

So what do we feel when we are reminded by illness and other mishaps that we are struggling survivors in a shattered world? I won't speak for you, but my tendency has been to get busy fixing things. And yet, I've learned by living that I'm really only a part of any solution. Any strength or wisdom I have for today's problems is supplied. I don't create it. It is granted by the Source, for momentary use.

All of which has me modifying my perspective. Because while my son lies sleeping upstairs on a cold school morning, Tamiflu and ibuprofen coursing through his otherwise robust young veins, I have the anonymous privilege of being alone with God. I can ask for His heart, His courage, His direction. When I release from feeling that I need to be the healer, then I somehow know God is repairing some things in me, too.

You may be in a spot like I am, in a tumultuous economy, fraught with worry and overextension, wondering about your health, your children's health, the future, college costs, your marriage, your life span, if you're making the world a better place. If you and I had coffee this morning and began listing things to worry about, we'd make ourselves sick before we finished one cup. I scan my snug but stained home and can instantly notice sagging cushions, dog-hair tumbleweeds, cracked walls, broken-water-pipe stains...mess. And we're living a cozy, tidy life by planetary standards. Rich in love and modern amenities. We eat well, attend school, work hard, have access to medical care, raise and enjoy two beautiful kids, donate to charities, and help in our community. But the point is, at any moment I could choose to only see how everything needs fixing. And suddenly, my oxygen intake squeezes, and my stress level rises. I feel to blame, driven, overwhelmed.

I suspect there is a Healer outside me who is far more able to carry this, or any greater kind of load, than I am. He's already carried me this far, for goodness' sake.

As I entrust my decisions to His leading and turn away from self-deprecation, I deepen and widen my relationship with God. This quest I am on, to escape the weight of supermom myths that seize my worth, is slowly morphing toward a tiny Scripture verse I tucked in my heart years ago: "Pray continually" (1 Thessalonians 5:17 NIV).

Entrusting your decisions to God's leading and turning away from self-deprecation widens and deepens your relationship with God.

Why is it that the invitation of this verse can seem so difficult, frightening…even oppressive? Because we are wired to desire freedom. Little do I know yet that all God's wisdom, even the commandments, free me from the alternative of going blindly my own way. Without supernatural peace. Without selflessness. Without forgiveness. Without gratitude.

Can I wager that the reason we moms are

fixated on fixing all the wrongs in our world is that we tend to simultaneously worry and want release from worry? Thus, we bind ourselves so tightly it causes a chronic wounding.

I don't know about you, but I've been yelled at on more than one occasion by those I love most to "Stop trying to fix it and just listen!" When will I trust that this life is an adventure in letting go of control and opening to others? As the nurturers, built a bit softer and gentler by nature, moms like us are great at holding, kissing, crying with, bandaging, and back rubs. But what I want to reach for knowing in my core is that I did not decide to do any of that apart from God. If every day I'm given becomes an envelope filled with time to do as God wills, then each day is well lived, even if it involves tragedy, breakups, broken bones, or apparent failures and valleys. Who would I think I'm kidding, anyway? Do I think God doesn't know His world is fractured? Do I think I am the one who extends life eternally? Do I think I can paint on a face that He won't see my soul through? To begin the process of allowing God into all my unfixed areas, I offer this prayer:

Dear Heavenly Father, this life as I know it will not continue as is. Every day, I march toward an unknown death and worry about making good on so many things before I am remade as a

Heavenly being I cannot comprehend. Today and every day, will You show me in Your immeasurable, unpredictable way that You know all this is happening and Your plan is unshakable and well? Help me, each day, to not miss the miracle or contentment in small, abiding, even tedious tasks. To remember that Your life force is deep in the soil and infinitely upward into forever. That even You, in all Your mighty power, delicately form a sprout beneath a stone. That You care about every detail. That each of us is loved and that You, not I, will fix what may seem unsalvageable, in Your good time. Help me be a vessel for Your refreshing hope and peace. I only am given today. Use me to fix what You will, not what I can alone. I'm messy. But You knew that. Show me, carry me, guide me. In Jesus' name, Amen.

So today, when my husband unpacks his demanding day, when fever continues, when my daughter attends to her busy life, I will attempt to offer tranquility instead of solutions. I will relax my eyes, soften my stature, and listen to my own needs as well. If a hot bath is possible and in order, I will reject the guilty breath of the enemy and replace it with trust. If any grief is too weighty, I will offer it back up to God. Yet if I career into losing it instead of choosing what's best, I can also reach out for forgiveness. God is always doing a new thing.

The truth is every one of us is worthy. Our

part is to live and reflect that. I am not God, but I believe Him. There are issues I cannot heal, but I can learn more about how God handles jealousy, poverty, accusations, meanness, prejudice, affliction, rejection, murder, and so much more by listening to Him in the flesh, through the words of Jesus. I can be a lifelong disciple and invite others to learn from Him as well. Jesus doesn't tell us to fix everything but to help inspire more learners by sharing our true-life story of hope. He doesn't tell us to set records straight or get revenge, but rather to make amends and lean on Him for the victory. To love.

In fact, I think Jesus summed up our calling beautifully in the verse referred to as "the greatest Commandment" in Matthew 22:37–40 NIV, Jesus replied, "Love the Lord your God with all your heart and with all your soul and with all your mind. This is the first and greatest commandment. And the second is like it: Love your neighbor as yourself. All the Law and the Prophets hang on these two commandments."

God doesn't tell us to set records straight or get revenge, but to make amends and lean on Him for the victory.

Notice carefully that it doesn't say to copy

your neighbor. Warn your neighbor. Impress your neighbor. Exceed your neighbor. No, it offers simply the work of loving. Further, because God speaks uniquely to each one of us, I happen to prefer what I feel is an even sharper version of this commandment. In John 13:34–35 NIV, Jesus simply says, "A new command I give you: Love one another. As I have loved you, so you must love one another. By this everyone will know that you are my disciples, if you love one another."

I like two words in this verse most of all: 1) *new*, and 2) *love*.

Every day is a new chance to muster it up inside you. I know the I-can-fix-it-all myth needs to be rewritten in my heart, but I am not yet immersed enough in daily application to turn this around. So today, I am deciding to do my part in advancing God's healing in His time by doing what is loving. Or trying to, anyway, without perfection. I will heat the soup and pour the cough syrup and refill the water, but I am not in charge of the miracle. I am a thankful witness. What good does it do to be put on a pedestal and become my own false idol? Or anyone else's, for that matter? Why should I take pride in centering anyone's worship on the wrong authority?

My wish is that all the "fixers" like me could enjoy more and stress less. It won't make complications disappear, just less capable of killing our souls. At any time, anyone can ask our God, "Speak into my soul what You would have me do next. Show me and allow me a feeling of conviction as You lead." If it feels right, even if slightly or terribly uncomfortable, it's likely from God. If it's the loving thing to do, it's likely your next best move. If something feels dishonest, shady, fake, or wrong—not just intimidating— it's likely from the enemy. Even if you don't know what in the world to choose, ask God to move your heart and hands. Beyond fear, but not beyond hope and honesty.

For example, a wonderful woman I admire told me this story:

I was teaching first grade at a private school. It was the last day, and I came home laden with books, papers, and a lot of junk. It was also the last day for public school, and all four of my children as well as my husband were there waiting for me. When I walked in the door, my husband announced excitedly that we were driving to Quebec, Canada. We were going now! Of course, my family was excited over the prospect of a new adventure. I wanted nothing more than to unload my burden and sit down for a while with a cup of coffee. My mind started racing: What would we wear, who packed, where were we staying? None of those questions were answered. Not one. In that moment, I could have stood firm and said, "Like heck we're going to Quebec!" Instead, I gave the whole adventure over to God. And thankfully, we had a wonderful time. We toured Montreal, Quebec and even stopped in Ottawa on the way home. Had I not chosen in that moment to let God lead instead of fixing it the way I wanted it, I would have missed out on some pretty sweet memories.

Writing this book is a case in point for me. Many days, I couldn't find time. Many days, I'd find anything else to do in the open hours I did have. Now, the more I write through it, the more I realize it isn't mine anyway. The times I jumped right into it productively were the times that God thought it was best to use me for it.

Other times, He had something else for me: chauffeuring, cooking, cleaning, working, et cetera.

I have to believe, for moms everywhere, that we are not able to fix it all. However, we are supporting the sacred healing process when we fix our expectance and adoration on God and the time-tested truths found in His Word.

Staring at my laptop's boot-up screen, I soak in my chosen screen saver. It reads, "Things do not get better by chance, they get better by change." This little thought vibrates with complexity. First, the concept of *better*. Isn't *better* different in the heart of each beholder? And really, isn't change the only unavoidable constant? Isn't this asking me to view life as purposely improving? What it actually speaks to me with every visit to the keyboard is, "Take some kind of action today. Don't be just passive. Participate. Don't believe it's all random garbage. Take up my cross and follow." See Matthew 16:24 NIV.

To simplify with one example, if my head is pounding, I need to take action to hydrate, breathe deeply, or rest. When I feel less pain intensity, I can better serve. Why the inner clawing, then, each time I read it, that I am not changing correctly, or fast enough, or well enough? Is surreality infecting society with the presumption that we need to fit a more general, poorly constructed mold defined for us by someone other than God?

So I ask for wisdom. I hear that it's a wise idea to notice and celebrate when things get better by my definition. My physical fitness won't improve overnight, but the way I approach it now is better for my age and life today. And that has changed every decade. I rode my bike so furiously last summer, like someone ten or more years younger than I am, that I managed to throw my neck and shoulders right into physical therapy and chiropractic care. My numb arms took months to heal. Now, chiropractic, massage, and yoga are new practices I will strive to fold into my new direction. I have changed. To something better for me. In this, I see a kind of epiphany.

Should I, then, stop thinking all things or anything could ever be fixed by me? And rather, change little things I do to different things that I sense God pointing me toward? Is this how to participate in continual healing?

For me, this comes with a central certainty that I learned in Beth Moore's Book of Daniel study (*Daniel: Lives of Integrity, Words of Prophecy*). My core takeaway from this work is that God promises that He is the deliverer. He is a promise keeper. So whenever there is a fiery trial of any kind—hot as a furnace, even—He will indeed deliver me one of three ways—away from it, through it, or by it into His eternal arms. This is especially poignant when passing through times of disease, death, divorce, and destruction.

With this wisdom, I can know that even if it's killing me, it won't be this way forever. So what do we ever fix? Doesn't that connote a permanency? Is there anything outside the law of transformation?

Author Richard Bach is quoted as saying "What the caterpillar calls the end of the world, the master calls the butterfly."

So in our physical life—this life that allows for a worldly death and heavenly transformation—we can actually allow lots of little deaths along the way as practicing our faith. When something is in a state of chaos and I want to take credit for fixing it because I'm desiring supermom status, maybe I'd do better to acknowledge, admit, and be present in the confusion and believe it is part of an unavoidable transformation. If I remain open, loving, and trusting, how can I stand in my own way? I can let God steer both me and the situation. Then, thankfully, I can give the credit to Him.

> *When I want to take credit for fixing because I'm desiring supermom status, maybe I'd do better to acknowledge the chaos and confusion and believe it to be part of an unavoidable transformation.*

Right now, in the preschool where I work, we are teaching the children Psalm 27:1. With hand motions upward, then outward, finished with an adorable shrug, their tiny voices collectively pronounce, "God is my light and my salvation. Whom shall I fear?" It makes me aware that most of my fix-it frustration is based in fear, to be sure. God, help me remember the unfailing strength of what is true.

After rolling these thoughts around in my heart in the presence of the Holy Spirit, I'm sensing that the new truth beyond this I-can-fix-it-all myth may sound something like this:

Rather than quickly fixing, I can patiently participate in the process of transformation.

for individual reflection
or group discussion

1. Have you ever tried to fix a crisis or issue in your life without giving it completely to God?

2. How quick are you to advise and mend rather than pray and listen?

3. Can you recall a time when you sensed divine intervention was creating a solution for you? What did God lead you to do as part of the solution?

4. Why are we uncomfortable with having problems we know are simply part of the human experience?

5. What are some good things to say to yourself or favorite Scriptures to lean on as you allow situations to heal in God's time, doing only what you are able?

6. What could happen if you let a problem go along without your trying to fix it? Have you ever tried praying your way through something outside your ability to repair?

7. Could just listening without offering to fix things be part of a solution?

8. What is one problem you can work on fixing and one you can pray back to your Creator?

5

living in truth and grace

Do not conform to the pattern of this world, but be transformed by the renewing of your mind. Then you will be able to test and approve what God's will is—his good, pleasing and perfect will.

—Romans 12:2 (NIV)

You did it. You waded in the muck of four myths that are binding hearts and souls. With you, I'm praying we're brave enough to reframe each of our own negative former patterns, opening to the authenticity that love fosters.

If you're like me, some of the exercises suggested in the balance of this book will stick, and some will take revisiting and reworking. Use them as a springboard for your own fresh ideas. Try some as an exercise in rewriting the way you do you. The goal for me is to be more like Jesus and less like the sins of the world. All while admitting I will never be Jesus or perfect. Or super.

I just want to be less superficial and more who I was created to be. Part of a plan, not in charge of it. You and I are miracles God thought enough of to create and weave into His story. So let's revisit the myths we have unwound together.

You and I are miracles God thought enough of to create and weave into His story.

Instead of striving to have it all, we can say to our souls, *"I have all I need today, thanks to the grace of God."*

Instead of stressing to do it all, we can admit, *"I can do what I choose to do in this moment, God willing."*

Instead of wanting to be it all, we can rest in knowing that *"I contribute to God's plan by simply being who I am."*

And before we trample others with selfish fix-it-all solutions, we can remind ourselves, *"I can patiently welcome the process of transformation rather than quickly fixing things."*

But how do we live out this new perspective? With humility. Showing grace. Speaking our reality. Sharing love. In the chapters that follow, you will find homegrown, modest suggestions for keeping it real.

part two

cultivating peace:
quick and easy
practices for
your new perspective

6

lay down your cape

No one lights a lamp and puts it in a place where it will be hidden, or under a bowl. Instead they put it on its stand, so that those who come in may see the light.

—Luke 11:33 (NIV)

What super-accessory are you hiding within? Is it holding you back?

Is it that career you always knew you would master? The perfect kids you always swore you would raise? Is it your unreasonable commitment to your superhuman ability to never, ever lose it in the face of any issue your children blindside you with? I don't know why it happens, but we moms can unwillingly weave a heavy costume fashioned from our unwarranted expectations, fears, comparisons, and circumstances.

One of the most critical steps, I believe, in becoming free to live in God's truth—all the while receiving and offering grace—is to lay something down that I've been clutching desperately. My career, my dreams, my mirror's reflection, my social standing, my tightly linked cape of overexertion. My supermom ability to swoop in and fix all my kids' issues. My justifications of all the things I chase with a gnawing emptiness.

I distinctly remember laying down one of my capes after pushing through our first two physically demanding fixer-uppers to the first time we built new. I had climbed and sweated up the ladder of "well-ordered home" until I no longer trusted anyone to accept any of my imperfect reality. Even my messes, as a supermom who kept a super-tidy house, had to be small, folded, piled, and arranged. I put everything away faster than it could be enjoyed. I drove myself away from self-care and peace with a maniacal need to look put together should anyone drop by for a playdate. Years into these exhausting shenanigans, I finally burned out. I retired my bathroom-cleaning supplies. I dropped my cape. I simply couldn't keep it up. I remember saying to my husband, regarding keeping our house spic-and-span, "That's no longer my passion." Of course, what also factored into to my decision was my awareness of a whisper that there was a passion much better suited to me. And a freedom that God desired for my heart.

By laying down our self-made capes (which, of course, we don't actually wear—it's just that, unfortunately, everyone can sense when we have them on), then you and I are allowing others not to feel what we want them to feel. To simply do the work of feeling what God is speaking to you or to me. Our real jobs, in other words.

The best way I can think to lay down my cape is to close my eyes and picture untying its bind around my neck. Letting it tumble in folds to the floor. As it falls, I can see it melting like all proverbial wickedness when doused with a refreshing splash of what is truly good. Or I envision removing a mask and sharing secrets. Yes, it makes me feel vulnerable. Like walking into a room full of gossips. I now have to accept that I am not as good as God who supplies my insight, my safety rope, my sail, my boat on the water. I am free to admit that there is a better captain, whose guidance gives me life.

Try in your own way to lay something down that is suffocating you. Visualize a releasing of some kind that works for you. Do it again and again as needed. Ask God to show you—to define for you—what is concealing your light. Pray for His help to let it go. A friend of mine nutshelled it like this for me: "Don't know how to parent these kids? Ask the One who made them!"

I don't believe that humility is self-belittling or feigned unworthiness but rather an enlightened joy. Deep delight that not only is it not all up to me, but that it simply couldn't be. You see, what was obscured by my discarded cape is a master-crafted, three-dimensional, living puzzle piece in the great mystery of life. It includes scars, shattered parts, and current wounds. It was designed by God with images, angles, colors, cuts, and a shape that only I can offer. And the same is true for you. Because if we, indeed, are each one part of a body of Christ, then shape-shifting to please the world's view will decrease the intended seamless

> *Try in your own way to lay something down that is suffocating you. Ask God to show you what is concealing your light.*

beauty of humankind. We are not shaped to fit in unrecognizably or to stand out in selfish opposition, but to discover our sacred design and together form a greater, unimaginably glorious masterpiece.

I now see that my former must-be-a-supermom cape, which I'm more likely to roll up in like a security blanket, was asphyxiating me. As I require others to validate me, I lose focus on the One who is trying to reach, lead, and renew me.

Do it today. Lay down what's not so helpful or not working out for you, or kick off the bowl or basket you're figuratively hiding under. Take off the mask. Let your costume dissolve. Step out of the hindrance of into His light. We are God's. Protected by a power that no superpower can supersede or diminish.

Just read through Psalm 139 and you will know that, to the One who matters, you are visible, valuable, and victorious. No wonder-woman feats, stunts, or getup required.

for individual reflection
or group discussion

1. What feels ill-fitting to you when you sense a striving to be super?

2. What can you imagine laying down?

3. In what area would you be willing to confess to being vulnerable or lacking?

4. Describe the real you. How do you feel most free? Most loved? Most loving? Most capable?

7

let go of yesterday's worries

So don't worry about these things, saying, "What will we eat? What will we drink? What will we wear?" These things dominate the thoughts of unbelievers, but your heavenly Father already knows all your needs.

—Matthew 6:31–32 (NLT)

I adore the section in the Book of Matthew, from 6:25 through 35, subtitled in some versions with a very direct "Do Not Worry" and in others as "The Cure for Anxiety." Well, sure.

What good will it actually do to be anxious and worry? But somehow, these lines in God's love letter feels like He knows exactly how I'm made. And that, naturally, I am going to worry.

Worry is one of the enemy's many tools. When you feel it rising up, it carries a power that feels counterproductive—destructive, even—to the peace supplied by faith. (See Romans 5:1.)

I'm no theologian, but I know faith gives me a toolkit. It's neatly itemized for us in Ephesians 6:14–18 as a belt, breastplate, gospel, ready feet, shield, helmet, and sword. So when I let the troubles of my past take over driving me into my future, I'm willingly tossing out this journey's road-safety kit and drifting toward danger.

I don't believe we won't worry, any more than I believe life is trouble free. I just want to stand in firm opposition to reactivating my past worries and giving them undeserved authority over today's possibilities. I confess to being pretty bad at this discipline because I have a tendency to stack up my worries of the past as a bastion against worries to come. As if I've not survived those old worries. As if I'm not forgiven, able to forgive, loved, trying, and still alive.

Do you do this? Do you worry that because last time you tried to do something brave and were embarrassed, this time, God's calling should be avoided? Worry that because someone you love has hurt you in the past, this now renders you unlovable? Worry that because you haven't kicked that habit yet, you never will? Worry that because someone you love has gone astray, you'll never reach them? Worry that because someone prefers you a certain way, you'll lose them (and everyone else for that matter) if you change? Worry that because you've lost control or management of an area of your life (career, home, parenting, etc.), you'll never regain any stability? Or that all will judge your new lacking in this area?

I'm hoping that together we can let our past be a story—not a sentence—with all-new pages unfolding. It starts today, this moment. And, as I said at the beginning of this section, this will likely take revisiting, renewing, and countless retakes. But I'm believing with you that God makes everything new. And although we are improved and possibly matured by hard choices, calamities, and trials, we are not stymied by them. We are not smothered by them, but rather, standing despite them. On top of them. Today belongs to

Today belongs to each one of us, ripe with potential miracles.

each one of us, ripe with potential miracles.

Doesn't His Word wake us to the fact that not one of us can add an hour to our lives with worry? (Matthew 6:27 NIV). I think we should tell worry to take a hike. I think we should instead go ahead and hope. Take action. Save up for something you dream about, apologize to that person whose forgiveness you need, ask for help, whatever you feel will show you what could happen without worry in your way. I'm not claiming that refusing to worry is a magic trick for problem-free living, but I just can't find any productivity in worrying. Why not try flipping worries, one by one, on their heads? Turn each one around with your own mental positivity. If you're worried about an unknown fearful outcome, film your own mental movie of the best possible scenario. Because something happened last time and you can't unsee it, challenge yourself to see it going differently this time. Give your worries to Jesus, and trust him to turn them into blessings.

The past is not the present or the future. It belongs behind you. With you, wiser, seeing a better way forward.

for individual reflection
or group discussion

1. Can you name an old worry to which you give undeserved attention or power?

2. Read Psalm 118:24. How can you help yourself proclaim, if even silently, that God made this very day with a purpose for you?

3. Can you recall a time you fought back worry and talked yourself into a better place?

4. In hindsight, what worries has God taken care of for you?

5. It's been said, "Worrying won't stop bad things from happening. But it will stop you from enjoying the good things." Is there an area of your life you're missing out on because of worry?

8

let prayer replace
your sabotaging self-talk

Prayer is simply a two-way
conversation between you and God.

—Billy Graham

I follow an awesome blog, lovingly served up
by a holistic nutritionist who says, "Worrying
is like praying for things we don't want." What
a concept! Following on the heels of our worry
chapter—if worrying can be considered a
form, albeit warped, of prayer—imagine how

worry-free prayer could have a redirecting force on our runaway worry train.

So what to do instead of worrying as a slim-chance, griping attempt at prayer? Pray for help. Instead of self-deprecation and shaming? Pray. Instead of regretting and despairing? Pray. If there is any chapter that gets to the heart of this book's dream for you, it is this one. Prayer is the life-giving oxygen supply connecting you and your Creator. It is your way to wisdom. We've likely all heard the speech about putting on your own air supply first so you are able to help your kids put on theirs. Talking to yourself is infused with a whole lot more opportunity for fruitfulness when preceded by talking to your Maker.

Prayer is the life-giving oxygen supply connecting you and your Creator. It is your way to wisdom.

God knows. He knows what you're worried about because you've been given the gift of shepherding the lives He bore through you. He knows what's happened to your body since becoming a mom. He knows what fears you're grappling with as your children struggle and grow. He knows what you're happy about. He designed what thrills you, even if it seems silly to others. He wants you to be you, completely.

To be the mom you want to be. And to be honest with Him. There are no lies God can't see through. And no greater love. When you find yourself whipped up in an anxiety-ball of "Where did I go so wrong?" grab your replacement. Grab on to the One who stood in your place. Who knows every terror imaginable. Who allows the capacity for pain in this world to whittle us holy. Replace the mean, scary, stressful things you say to yourself with the surrender of prayer.

Ask God, "What are You doing? Show me."

Ask yourself, "What do I love?" It matters. Be truthful. The answers are there. Prayer is how you dig in and get to them.

Replace self-talk like "Why am I such a loser?" with a prayer of your own. I can't stress enough that it has to be *your own*.

One I might use is this:

God, I know You see me struggling to accept this role I've chosen. Show me how it is right and within Your plan. Or show me what You want me to choose instead. Give me the peaceful trust to know I will recognize that it's from You. Speak to me about the goodness of this station I'm in. Or give me the road signs out of it. Give me a word today to carry me afloat above it.

I know you've heard this next bit before. And still, it's worth repeating. Don't pretty up your prayer. That's hiding. And don't leave out stuff you don't want God to see or hear. That's pretending.

If you want the power of prayer to replace your current self-talk, believe that God will supply. He will supply what I personally believe is the very best outcome of prayer. He will return to you peace.

This is not a microwave moment. You know God is still performing miracles of the "Shazam!" variety all around His planet, but prayer is not a pill. It is a plan for your heart. A positioning. Not of trying really hard, but of trusting really hard. Whenever your falsely scripted self-talk starts taking over, give it to God in prayer. Even if it begins, swells, and ends with fury. Releasing it to the One who made you deflates its power to destroy you. He made you. He's not shocked. And He can handle it.

for individual reflection
or group discussion

1. What is your most pressing need right now? Write a prayer that gives it to God for healing.

2. What do you tend to say to yourself that doesn't sound like how God feels about you? Does your family notice this and point it out to you?

3. How could refusing to self-sabotage help you enjoy being a mom more?

4. How would it feel to say good things about yourself to yourself? How could you teach your children to try it?

5. Consider one area in which you sabotage yourself with mean-speak. What could you say instead that would be uplifting, empowering, freeing?

9

get to know (and love) yourself

Today you are You, that is truer than true.
There is no one alive who is You-er than You.

—Dr. Seuss

It's a little scary to begin a chapter that feels like rushing headlong into the ocean of Pinterest commandments to be this, be that, do this, do that. Being told to be myself is as encouraging as it is discouraging. Is this true for you? Well, part of our pilgrimage together, if we are to shed the stranglehold of false pressures, would be to work hard at listening within. It will involve tilling up dead spots in our lives to gain wisdom from our Maker as to who He made—and is making—each one of us to be. So, please, before I fumble forward, I'm asking your forgiveness for any encouragement from me that just feels like more demands on you. I'm a work in progress, and my passion has fast legs. I am learning and trying right along with you.

The sheer variety of God's creation convinces me that God did not intend for you or me to be anything less than 100 percent inimitable originals. Some of the fun in life is surely found imagining His loving thoughts over the uniqueness of you—His handiwork—and then joining Him in enjoying that. But what a tumultuous quest. Like a ship bobbing in a squall at sea, we amuse and disgust ourselves, nurture and reject ourselves, better and injure ourselves. If the search for truth and grace is worthwhile, how truthful can we be? And how much grace will carry us?

As I sat in the chemical- and rubber-scented lobby of a local auto center waiting for the privilege of road-ready tires, I was gifted with a wall-size window through which I could see the rain pelting down and feel protected enough to pour out my confusion onto paper. I felt on the one hand served and on the other, enslaved.

Stuck in a mundane maintenance task but immeasurably thankful. Isn't that how finding ourselves feels? Like, ugh, we don't want or have time to, but if we are to roll out safely, we must?

I know I am not the only mom who longs to be myself, but that longing is tempered continually by the admission that someone else knows better. Our challenge is to tune our individual souls to wisdom that matters: to the only One who defines each one of us. Then we hold on with every fiber to the fact that He fits us all together, each needing the gifts of others. Years of mercy have taught me that no mortal is perfection. We are made by a perfect God. Faults, temptations, shortcomings, doubt, and all. I don't believe God made us to hurt, stress, sabotage, or drive ourselves. But I do those things anyway. Do you? This is why there's a chapter in this book called "Get to Know (and Love) Yourself." Not so that it stops there, but so that it doesn't get stopped up. So you can regain and claim your flow that blesses.

Scripture makes it clear: we love because He first loved us (1 John 4:19 NIV). Love is how God made us, it's what He is teaching us, it's how He equips us. Running from that love because you don't think you deserve it or don't have time for it essentially renders the love you give away disingenuous. How are you filling up?

From what living source? Into what do you dip your cup of grace that can then truly overflow to others?

I'm not suggesting that we stifle our souls with self-interest. I'm just offering that what makes you feel more loved, balanced, able, patient, ready, honest, energetic, or kind is a good pursuit. It is simply not smart to squelch your every desire. Indeed, we need to listen in mediation with God to discern the goodness and life in our desires. If it builds your capacity for service by relaxing your frazzled grip, I'm suggesting you try it as "you time."

In essence, we are a planet tending to run from ourselves. We death-clutch our devices, staring downward to avoid human contact, killing ourselves to reply to too many one-dimensional e-interruptions. To get real requires a slowing down. A prayer about our roots. Is God's purpose in making me that my feigned perfection can fool others to put faith in me? I prefer that my imperfect reliance on His guidance puts others' faith in Him.

We are all of us along for the ride, not authoring the map. And I strongly suggest that some essentials are in order. (Oh no, please forgive my directives.) Get sleep. Take care of your health. Laugh at life's surprises, and ask

God to help you be you. You are a bundle of one-of-a-kind gifts that only you received. As the famous saying goes, "You don't have to be pretty like her. You can be pretty like you." If long walks give you time to assess and explore your gifts—go there. If baking cakes lifts you to share them—do that. If digging in the earth gives you peace to discover and appreciate how you're made—allow that. Not always, I know. But certainly not never. What is it that makes you feel like your own signature? Put it into words, and make time for it.

> *What is it that makes you feel like your own signature? Put it into words, and make time for it.*

The more effort you put toward acknowledging what feels fulfilling and joyful to you, the more your kids, your husband, and you can know one another. Do your children know what delights you? Do you? Please do it, on purpose. And do less and less of what robs you of your joy.

Best of all, love that about yourself. I promise you, the world needs it.

for individual reflection
or group discussion

1. Ask yourself, "What are my guiding principles?" For example, mine are to be 1) honest, 2) genuine, and 3) caring. What three to five attributes make up your soul? What are you doing in your life that expresses these? Acknowledge these actions as success.

2. What can you decide to like about yourself? How does it help others around you get better?

3. What hobby is uniquely you, and what time frame can you write on your calendar for it? Even and especially if it means erasing commitments you're not truly interested in pursuing.

4. Pray this with God until you find answers that feel counter-cultural, unpolished, and unrehearsed: "God, what do I really want that is Your will?" Then appreciate what you are doing, have done, or will do to achieve that.

10

listen for God on purpose

It is written: "Man shall not live on bread alone, but on every word that comes from the mouth of God."

—Matthew 4:4 (NIV)

How are you going to get to know and love yourself if you're not desperately seeking what God wants for you?

I'm pretty certain you know you were made for something beyond yourself—because He made you a mom! That's a really great way of showing you that He trusts your ball of tangled mess to do something eternally crucial. And guess what: God didn't just make your kids; he made *you*. With every sin tendency, bad habit, weakness, perceived limitation, and oddity that makes you necessary. Also, with every bit of potential, willingness, talent, gift, and desire you own or develop.

Every one of us moms can find fleeting happiness in anything easy and fun that borders on careless as a temporary relief. But He wants to give us much more. He wants us to experience the deep, lifesaving joy of sacrifice. He has a peace for us that comes from a place beyond self-satisfaction.

This is the peace I want moms to trust-fall into as we go ahead and discover and declare what gets our juices flowing. There are way too many *shoulds* and *musts* out there to choke us all on the business of the world. But why? Is the competitive, success bandwagon a good ride? Are we so focused on being just like or better than a competitor that we risk dilution?

I wonder if that gnawing feeling of unfulfillment or "misfit-ness" is not only because we give and serve and focus on others to our detriment, but also because we give and serve to compete, not to collaborate. Because doing is the thing. As fast and furious as visibly possible. On all the same social media channels. In all the same stores. In all the same groups and schools. Heck, we now have an actual dictionary word for this new phenomenon: FOMO. Look it up, because lots of us are living it. It's defined "anxiety that an exciting or interesting event may currently be happening elsewhere, often aroused by posts seen on social media." And, here's the example sentence given: "I realized I was a lifelong sufferer of FOMO." Feeling like you must be doing at all times what everyone else is busy doing is not a satisfying thing. It's a suffering thing.

You don't need to do what every other mom is doing because you'll lose sight of His way for you.

What about listening to what really, truly moves you alone? I'm betting that if any of us moms step forward courageously, right into the middle of our figurative rivers at flood stage with a faith like Joshua, into what feels good and right and helpful, we will begin to feel an inward calm. You see, there's actually a whole lot of insecurity stuffed up inside our longing to be supermoms. Security is actually found in the anonymous conviction that God made you the way He did on purpose. You don't need to do what every other mom is doing because you'll lose sight of His way for you.

Let me show you how God can plant this inclination in your heart, through a true story shared by a mom I interviewed for this book. She is passionate about trusting what God has to say to you privately. As a young career woman, before taking on the added demands and distractions of parenting, this mom was given a gift that continues to guide her as she makes her mom decisions. She was on the West Coast, working and taking a class for about a year. For eight months she took the same route to and from her class, to avoid having to brave the L.A. freeway system and stress out her already-overwhelmed inner compass. You may share this fear with her. I know I do. When new places disrupt our life patterns, my fear about being directionally-challenged rears its whiny voice over my peace. I tend not to trust that I'll find my way. I'm terrified of getting lost. I look for slower, safer roads.

She, too, drove the same route every day because it was the first route she tried, and it was becoming familiar. Every day she avoided the trap of unknown highways.

Yet one day, out of the blue, as she was

driving along, she felt a strong conviction—a voice of direction—telling her to take the left that would send her onto the freeway. As she described it, there was traffic and not much time, and the sense of pressure mounted. She knew God was trying to lead her. Yet, out of fear, and a presumed sense of control, she ignored it.

Lo and behold, as she continued up the road to take the left she'd taken for months toward home, she was pulled over by the police. By an officer who sat waiting at a posted sign, that in her repetitive commute, she had never noticed. The sign at her usual left turn read: No Left Turn between 4 and 6 p.m. Now, I know you know what time it was. To this day, she says, she will never know if the sign was new, or she finally just got unlucky along a course not meant for her. Nonetheless, she was hit with a $250 fine and having to pay for driving school. A painful expense at any age, and not exactly the thing one might call a God thing.

But to her, it still is. This was the catalyst that emboldened her to go a different way. The new way, God was cautioning her, that was the best way for her. The way that she at first allowed her fear to trump. The way she knew she was being guided, but ignored.

The beautiful outcome is that the next day,

as she braved that busy freeway for the first time, she actively noticed all the signs. She paid attention. And she easily, thanks to excellent signage, found her way back home. It was actually a smoother trip—and a shorter one. Saving her stress, time, and gas money.

The lesson she holds in her very personal box of heart-treasures, scripted by God for her alone, is to *trust that His way is always good*. She has learned that when you ask God to help you decide how to parent these kids, or love their Dad, you should listen well. Look for signs. And trust that what he puts on your heart with conviction may cost you something in the journey to learning your way—but it will actually be the easier way. His way. For you.

I realize that when you listen for what God created you to love, you may even have to leave a high worldly station. You may even do something radical. But you can hold your head up and know what you're finding is what you can pass on to your children.

You are listening for your purpose.

for individual reflection
or group discussion

5. Here's a great idea borrowed from Kyle Cease's hilarious book *I Hope I Screw This Up: How Falling In Love With Your Fears Can Change the World* (New York: North Star Way, 2017): Draw a line down the center of a piece of paper. On the left side, list what you would really love to do if you were truly being you. On the right side, write how you "Yeah, but I can't" yourself right out of doing it. Sit back and realize that every "Yeah, but" is actually you making a choice. How will you choose left-side living instead?

6. Write yourself a prayer that says, in your own words, "I'm off track, God, and not listening for You. Guide me toward doing what I love, and let that glorify You."

7. What is God trying to say to you right now that you know you are not listening to on purpose?

8. Make a list of the unique traits that God gave you. How do these make you a blessing to others?

11

listen to your kids on purpose

My dear brothers and sisters, take note of this:
Everyone should be quick to listen, slow to speak
and slow to become angry.

—James 1:19 (NIV)

When I prioritize listening for God's direction, I can truly say that the most tangible experience of clarity and peace I experience is when I then set aside my agenda and offer a gift of listening to either one of my kids. I suppose I would follow that with listening to my husband, listening to a friend, and listening to my extended family. Maybe the whole top quadrant of joy is realized in times of emptying and offering, involving eye contact and time. It's honestly when I feel a supernatural mending of previous arguments, misunderstandings, or missed opportunities. Actually, the point of this book is to pump up your listening practice by prioritizing God's quiet voice above all others.

I can't say, however, that I've mastered a single trick to muscle my ear in past the incessant obsession of technology. I honestly worry—hey, now, let's change that to *wonder*, right?—if the next generation will all exhibit "i-neck." That's my imagined skeletal/postural result of hours spent with heads bent down toward screens and handheld devices. Like a flower wilting in the face of a faux sun. I'm stupefied as to how to hold back the tsunami that is technology. But if I am to hang on to what's true, what have I enforced, encouraged, or done to limit the lure? What chores have I happily conquered while my kids were screening, as if tidiness were paramount to togetherness? Part of my inability is that God made me a loner. I value quiet and solitude. And darn it all, technology at home has made things quieter at times.

However, this still stands. If I ask my son and daughter to please look at me when they are preoccupied, they will. If I sit next to them and just *be* during their shows, games, or activities, they will eventually chat with me. Or they will ask me to please give them some alone time, which I completely respect. I treasure the renewal of sanctuary. But what I know equally is that our kids can get bottled up in their sanctuary with ideas and issues they don't think anyone else cares about.

Which reminds me of the Bible story in which Jesus fell asleep during the storm. As disciples feverishly tossed buckets of water overboard, they panicked: "Don't you care?" They did not ask, "Why aren't you doing something to help?" It's a basic need in each of our children to know that we care, not only that we're capable. In fact, I've stepped in to help handle issues with my son and, by doing so, pushed him further away. What he needs instead is for me to ask his opinion, to have him show me something, to listen to his new music, to look him in the eye.

And let's go here, Mom: If our kids are not listening to us, shouldn't we evaluate whether we're listening to them? Also, how about a new commitment that every listening session doesn't have to sting them back with a lesson from us?

Of the Internet-famous "seven things every child needs to hear" list, I think "I'm listening" is the most active. It requires even more patience and faith than "You can do it." If you haven't seen the list, here it is:

I love you.

I'm proud of you.

I'm sorry.

I forgive you.

I'm listening to you.

This is your responsibility.

You can do it.

You and I both know it feels weird. Deliberately halting our racing minds from forming all sorts of lists, to-dos, or reactions and just listening. With an "Oh wow!" or "That must be rewarding for you," or "Thanks for telling me about that," or simply "Tell me more." The end goal is that your child feels, in general, "I like talking to you," and "You don't frighten me."

I can tell you, as they get older, they will unload some stuff you do *not* want to hear. But where else do they take those seriously messy conundrums if not to you?

Here is another exercise to try. The next time you are receiving someone else's troubles, bad news, or overwhelming struggles, imagine how we walk together. Not actually inside one another's shoes, but beside them. So as I adjust my heart, I will figuratively and calmly plant my own two feet beside theirs. Because my first instinct, as I wrestle with that dastardly I-can-fix-it-all myth, is to assume responsibility for others' hardships. However, as part of this new journey, I will try instead presence over plans. To not formulate my response while listening. To not compare my troubles to theirs and plan my counteroffer. To resist mentally flipping through slots of availability on my calendar while listening. Because you see, our greatest deficit in this overstressed world is not time. We are not in need of more time to fit in more solutions. No, because we chase so much multitasking mania, the silent loss is the erosion of our attention. When walking beside someone, let's try to simply and totally...be. And allow inspiration to come whenever God decides.

Because we chase so much multitasking mania, the silent loss is the erosion of our attention.

Listening has to be authentic, not superficial.

They'll see right through it. But whatever way we start, let's start carving out more plain ol' relaxed listening time.

It's sure to remind us why we delight in our children, the way our heavenly Father delights in us.

for individual reflection
or group discussion

1. When was the last time you chose to simply listen to one of your children? How did it make you feel?

2. What gets in the way of active listening for you most often? Is there anything you can choose to let go or not do so you can find listening times?

3. Where does each of your children tend to open up most? In front of the TV? At bedtime? In the car? Can you be aware of each child's talkative time and resolve to spend five minutes of it just actively listening and receiving without forming a lesson?

4. Recall a time when someone really, authentically listened to you. How did it make you feel? Is that something you want your kids to feel?

12

let the truth be your strength

Strength comes from living your truth.
To be true and authentic is your path
to happiness, peace, and joy.

—anonymous

I've always told my kids, every time a new obstacle or trial threatens to run them down, "Remember, the truth is your strength."

Nothing other than what is actually true will sustain us.

People will judge, hate, neglect, abandon, hurt, test, and frighten us. Confusion, guilt, and immobility sneak their way in, right past a mind-set that's not eyes-wide-open on the truth.

My favorite source of truth is looking for what the Bible says on something. That's why I love listening to sermons, joining in Bible studies, and praying for answers. I once participated in a Priscilla Shirer study in which she set up a visual aid, stacking foam bricks higher and higher. Every time she added a brick, she said something hurtful or untrue that we moms tend to tell ourselves. It was disheartening to realize I was seeing my own complaints build that wall.

Then what she did so beautifully was knock that wall down. Brick by brick. With what the Bible says is true.

Think you're not special? The Bible says you are wonderfully made. Think you're stuck in your mistakes? The Bible says even while sinners, we are forgiven. The truth never gives out in its ability to convict us, redeem us, cleanse us.

Neither does honesty.

So when you're feeling like you don't

measure up to the supermoms you're surrounded by, speak truth into your soul. Or pray for it until you hear it silently. Clear away judgment, and focus on facts. Are you still standing? Do you serve a second-chance God? Are you odd and offensive, or are you a unique creation of a mysterious God? Does everyone look exactly alike? Is anyone ever perfect? Did you really say what so-and-so is saying you said? Is there time to try something new? Is there anyone who has not faltered in her job as a mom? Do your children know you love them? Is it OK to not enjoy what others are trying to persuade you to do?

It's amazing how much just focusing on the jewel of a word *true* will bolster your step, lift up your chin, and deepen your breath. My counselor calls it making decisions based on evidence.

> *Just focusing on the jewel of a word true will bolster your step, lift up your chin, and deepen your breath.*

I'm going to wager that something tends to happen to women when we become moms and play so many roles, that we sometimes feel dramatic. Things hurt more deeply because we're so tired. Things seem more critical because there are other lives involved. Dinners have to nourish. Kids should go to bed happy. But what is the truth? Only God is God. He made us fallible. And He gave us choice. Sometimes we choose what's truly best. Sometimes we miss the mark miserably.

As women, our feelings can get the best of us. I want to learn to embrace the facts. God sees what you are doing. God knows your struggle. God also knows your way out. Not one second of your mistakes, hurt, or pain will be wasted. The truth is that God makes beauty out of ashes. Just look at the evidence all around you.

Next time any mean girls or insensitive husbands or backbiting friend groups threaten your equilibrium, dive into what's true. For example, "A gracious woman gains respect" (Proverbs 11:16 NLT). Or "The wise woman builds her house, but with her own hands the foolish one tears hers down" (Proverbs 14:1 NIV). Try not to make it a practice to allow others to tear down the way you mother. And I need to remind myself that it's not constructive when I tear down my own house.

In every unforeseen situation we moms face, if it seems blurry, judgmental, deceptive, or scary, seek what's true. Hold on to it. Own it. The truth is your strength.

for individual reflection
or group discussion

1. Share a time when one of your children was hurt or afraid and you helped him or her define the truth in the situation. How did it help?

2. What is your favorite truth saying, quote, or Scripture? Do you keep it somewhere visible to others?

3. Get personal and specific. In your own words, list three truths that are worth living by for you.

13

stop trying to win

*For those who exalt themselves will be humbled,
and those who humble themselves will be exalted.*

—Matthew 23:12 (NIV)

I'm going to go right ahead and say that I'm sick and tired of hearing "Winning isn't everything; it's the only thing."

Would you try saying something unpopular, too?

I'd love if this book inspired someone to

say what they *really* feel is right and moral and healing and possibly not look like a winner in the process. You may just make some new friends, too. Others who are caught up in the ridiculousness but can't find a blinkin' olive branch to grab on to and scrabble to safety.

I'm not suggesting we run from risk or step out of the race marked out for each of us. Conversely, I mean to encourage the risk of leaping at our otherwise-missed chances to love.

If I am constantly worried about winning, and I can find no joy in any other state because winning is the only thing, I'm going to end up with a pretty thin life. My patience will be diminished by the stress of not seeing myself as being good enough unless I am officially better than that team, that committee, those neighbors, that sibling, that coworker, et cetera. Needing to be the winner easily haunts and tempts unwitting souls into lying, cheating, hurting, and ultimate emptiness.

Of course, everyone loves to have their hard work pay off. Putting in long hours of practice, days of proposal preparation, nights of studying—whatever the devotion and sweat invested—is sweetly rewarded by a win. Which is undeniably a good thing. Because when your heart and soul, guided by God and good intentions, work toward an honorable goal, I would agree that reaching that goal is a winning achievement.

What crushes our stability, however, is the need to win at all costs. Followed by boasting, even if silently. The need to win apart from fixing our eyes on Jesus. I'm talking about that insidious, imagined inner command to supersede others at the expense of reputation, self-control, health, friendships, or family, among many other gifts that are sacrificed in the race to win.

By suggesting that you let yourself off the hook in principle from always trying to win, I would love to practice being glad for others. Do we agree that jealousy for the sake of coveting is useless and non-beneficial? Jealousy if there is actual infidelity is understandable, but a great deal of jealousy comes from simply wanting. Wanting to win.

Couldn't it also be all right just to want to get better, to learn something, to enjoy the process, to foster some friendships, and to add to our variety of life experiences? Sincerely, I still don't know. And I'm guessing most of us don't either, for absolute certain. Because, unfortunately, we are competitive by nature. I think we'll always desire to win, keep, and shine.

So how do we temper that drive and cultivate

peace? It's a challenge to give your every effort into God's hands, but isn't it true that you and I have any chance to pursue any goal by the grace of God alone?

I find it interesting that as I poked around online for a definition of *win* and a definition of *victory*, it seemed to me that *win* implies coming in first position, in front of others. It seemed that *victory* is a triumphing over an enemy after a struggle. Maybe, then, it's OK to celebrate our own personal victories over our own particular inner lies and the enemy. Maybe we could see ourselves as battling off the enemy who wants to insult and weaken our mothering role. Instead of winning by having more, higher, better this and that than other moms, we can support each other in feeling victorious as we make tiny personal strides of improvement on our own unique home fronts.

Instead of winning, we can support each other in feeling victorious on our own home fronts.

I once heard that comparing and competing are decisions to determine your worth based on what others have, are, and do, when in reality, the only true measure is whether you are being you. Being consumed by winning says we don't matter unless we're the winner. It's likely that the real victory is within the familiar quote "Confidence is not in thinking yourself better, but in not having to compare yourself in the first place." Comparison makes us all the same, and you and I are created to be incomparable.

A simple way of stepping into our wanting nature for the day is to humbly offer up, "If not this, God, then something better."

Let's trying praying this more often.

And then let Him be the judge.

for individual reflection
or group discussion

1. You've heard the saying "Winners never quit, and quitters never win." Discuss or journal how it really makes you feel. Ask yourself how you might rephrase this. Don't make it perfect; just let it be personal.

2. Can you recall a time when you experienced what others may have seen as a loss but found something valuable in it?

3. What are some of the sneaky ways the world tempts us to try to win over others? Which one would you like to resist, in your own way, that would feel more peaceful to you?

14

practice praising over complaining

People won't have time for you if you are always angry or complaining.

—Stephen Hawking

We think it gives us power to point out what's wrong. Heck, I'm doing it in this book! Ugh. I assure you, though, the goal of this book is your peace and freedom. I'm not driven to give you assignments but rather to unload you. I aim to downsize. Simplify. Unwind.

Because it's in this state of release that our

frozen ruts become liquefied and we are lifted. Empowered to change course. Able to change the way we think or speak about things if we can't change them. Or, as one woman described it to me for this book, "brave enough to interrupt the pattern."

Here's an example of praising rather than pouting or marveling over moping. I interviewed a mom who explained that every day she has to take her large, arthritic dog for a walk. Every day, without fail. And what she has decided is to go with the flow of the day, reveling in the little things. Every day, she certainly could dream up a host of options more tailored to the world's standards of achievement than harnessing up a needy pet and taking his pace around the path.

The reality is that he often tires, and she winds up grounded. Utterly stuck. Because he's just too big to carry. So she makes a choice: one of the greatest graces God bestows.

In those moments, she has developed the practice of choosing praise over complaints. Wonder over worry. See, there are lots of fun ways you can catch-phrase it for your own application. The important thing is that good stuff happens when you do it. Instead of cussing, stressing, or remaining taut in the understandable grip of impatience while waiting for her dog's lungs and limbs to recover, she will look around for God's gifts. His unearned miracles that, although easy to rush past, hold the power to reset the soul.

She will focus on the gentle warm wind. An impossibly intricate wildflower. The resigned and trusting pant of a dog receiving healing from the ground's green coolness. In a state of stress, we miss the memories that fortify us. These snapshots of acceptance during moments in which we could feel stifled or powerless are ours to keep. They are times when gratitude can rush right in through the doors we open.

This chance to look for what to praise can happen anytime, anywhere. In the laundry room. At the pediatrician. While listening to your teens' current music choices in your car. While hearing your kids' papers read out loud. Any time you're mom-ing at an unselfish pace.

So when you're stuck in a relationship quandary, in the store getting school supplies, in traffic, in the bathroom with a sick child, or anywhere the tendency is to complain—look around for something to praise. Ask God to show it to you. Even better, say it out loud.

Think about how radical a love it would be if you focused on the good. If I can start, then it's possible it could become a habit. Instead of getting up remembering the things I can't stand about my current situation, I could focus on how handsome my husband is. I could focus on how that's one big reason we have the kids in the first place. It's a powerful handsome. I could focus on how my daughter is friendly instead of the times she is surly. I could worry less about my son's choices and notice choices he makes that are caring, responsible, and good. I'm guilty of overlooking these and focusing on what's bad. Because I'm a fixer.

Think about how radical a love it would be if you focused on the good.

If all I see is the bad stuff, how will I participate in cultivating the good? Will you try it with me? Praise hot showers. Your kids' energy. Free rainwater. Your legs, arms, breath. Praise your husband, please, for loving you. He and all these, and so much more, are gifts from the One who made you. If you have walked through the valley of losing or divorcing your husband, look for the good in that legacy and how it can shape your future. God was at work, holding you through all that, and He can help you find the good in it. You will have to look courageously with eyes you set free. Or if you just can't take a situation anymore, praise God for the inspiration to make it better so you can breathe.

With practice, you'll see more of what's good.
Even in the delays and detours, praise God.

for individual reflection
or group discussion

1. Think of a situation that's currently challenging you. What are some things this situation has revealed to you that are worth praising? Has it improved your patience? Has it made you stronger? Has it made you weak enough to ask for help and receive it?

2. Share a time when you made the choice to be glad in a situation that could easily make anyone mad. How did you choose? What was your internal dialogue?

3. List three of your top complaints. Can you reword them into praise? How does it feel in your soul as you do this?

4. List one good thing about your husband and each child. Tell them that you notice these things in them today. Note their reaction or response.

15

**choose *will* over *won't*
and *do* over *don't***

*For God has not given us a spirit of fear and
timidity, but of power, love, and self-discipline.*

—2 Timothy 1:7 (NLT)

This is such a simple concept it floors me. It's sort of like how Jesus distilled ages of sorrow into one powerful new command to love one another. Ah, but there's the catch. It's an easy concept in theory, harder to implement while parenting.

Sometimes, moms, we fight simplicity, don't we? We think surely this must be as complicated as it feels. That's based in our God-given ability to wrestle. He wants us equipped to battle our enemy. He wants us to wield His power within us. But we get our wires crossed by the world's messages. We start to believe the lies that we're not worthy. We start to think if we can't have it all, do it all, be it all, and fix it all, we may as well give up.

Here's the truth: you, my friend, are an overcomer. It's in you.

There are many ways God will guide you to live by the Spirit, so my suggestion in this chapter is to make two small word choices with big possibilities. I promise if you pick them up like free weights and work out with them, your resolve and optimism will grow.

> *Here's the truth: you, my friend, are an overcomer. It's in you.*

What I want moms to do is flip *won't* to *will* and *don't* to *do*.

For example, instead of "I won't eat any more sugar," say, "I will choose salad more often at mealtimes." Instead of "I won't be vulnerable to my husband anymore," say, "I will be vulnerable because I choose to be, and it's required for true intimacy." Instead of "I won't yell at my kids ever again," say, "I will see myself as patient and behave accordingly." What's more, instead of "Lia, don't just sit there," I could say, "Lia, what will you do now?"

Remember, a list of don'ts will naturally feel more negative than a list of dos. I'm guessing not many of us will actually make a list, just because that's how God made me. I'd like for moms to instead just catch ourselves when we make a negative demand that feels limiting, and flip it to a limitless positive.

Maybe that's actually why we say "I do" take this man's hand in marriage.

So right now, I'm going to try saying to myself: *I will laugh when I start taking everything so seriously. I will have hope. I will make mistakes and learn from them. I do have strength*, instead of *I don't have enough. I do have willpower.*

Sweet mama, you do, too.

for individual reflection
or group discussion

1. What are you currently denying yourself or disciplining yourself to avoid? Can you reword it as an "I will" or "I do" statement and see how that feels?

2. The next time you are teaching your children, try telling them what they can do instead of what they cannot do. For example, "Don't yell at me!" can flip to "You can lower your voice when we talk so I can stay calm." Instead of "Don't leave your towel on the floor!" try "Do remember to replace the towel so it's ready for your next shower." It may seem awkward, but it sure feels more gracious.

3. Be brave with me if you have kids who are teenagers or older. When one of your kids brings you a messy, even Satan-stronghold-level dilemma, will you try asking him or her, "What will you do?" If your child starts saying, "I can't" and "I won't," help him or her frame the response with "I can" and "I will."

4. Keep a journal of the times you flipped the script and benefited.

16

accept that all things are in process

What we call the secret of happiness is no more a
secret than our willingness to choose life.

—Leo Buscaglia

Confession: I pored over hundreds of
inspirational quotes and scriptures, trying to
find just the right golden nugget to capture the
essence of this chapter. I couldn't find it. Shown
above is a relinquishment: stop searching and
just choose. This quote from Leo Buscaglia is
good enough. And isn't that the grace I'm bent

to achieve? So I decided to live it myself. The upside is that the process taught me what I'm trying to say. In a day or two, heck, in an hour probably, I'll see, hear, or read just the right quote or Scripture that wraps up the immutable law of transformation perfectly. And I will let it be. Because everything is constantly happening.

Whether we're sleeping, sick, running, worrying, working, whatever; something is changing. Our temperature inside. The temperature outside. The mindset of someone we talked to last week. The length of our lawn. All things are continually in process. And what a revelation! If we really sink our teeth into that

Joy is fleeting and worth celebrating, pain is temporary, the sun returns, and tomorrow is coming in a completely unknown way.

juicy, delicious truth, we can know that joy is fleeting and worth celebrating, pain is temporary, the sun returns, and tomorrow is coming in a completely unknown way.

But oh, how we want control! How we want things to stay within our plan. Even, believe it or not, if they are not working out for our betterment or the betterment of those around us. There are many things I doubt, but of this I have proof. Even if I leave a room alone, untouched, unused, it gets musty. Leaves turn radiant without my involvement. Bulbs bloom and die and are reborn before my eyes. Children grow into adults, unstoppably. And infinite unseen things are continually in process.

Nothing is *not* changing.

Keep this shiny star in your pocket for reference: whatever you're going through will not remain exactly like this. Good or bad, this reminds us that good times are worth savoring, and bad times are not holding us hostage. Any one of you who've dropped off your babies at kindergarten, middle school, high school, or college for the first time knows exactly what I'm saying here. Our kids and what they need from us change so quickly it's tear-jerking.

Each of us can, indeed, decide to change in ways, while at the same time, we are all changing in ways outside our control. Cells split, winds thrash, water rises, the world turns. But tomorrow is new. Every single time. Brand new. Absolutely never a carbon copy of the day or the slate or the plan before it.

The Bible promises us that God is a master of renewal. His love creates, restores, and recreates. So hold on. And let go. Allow yourself to change, your needs to morph, and your views to bend, while listening closely for God's voice within. Because if something seems too hard to withstand, you can count on this: it's going to change. And if you place that pile of troubles in God's capable guidance, it will improve. Maybe not by worldly judgments but by the unchanging promise of divine change.

for individual reflection
or group discussion

1. Take a physical or mental walk. What has changed in your world in the last month? The last decade? Did you foresee all these changes, or do you see how change surprises you?

2. How are you changing in ways you love? What can you celebrate today about change you see in you?

3. Who do you know whose life is experiencing a lot of pronounced change lately? How can you offer them inspiration or commendation for how they are handling it?

4. Write down three praises on transformation in your marriage, your work relationships, your family, or a critical area of your life—and thank someone who walked with you through to this changed place.

5. What can you let go of and see what God can do with it?

a final word: wisdom

Ask, and it will be given to you; seek, and you will find; knock, and the door will be opened to you.

—Matthew 7:7 (NIV)

Thank you for your heart. For your loving, compassionate willingness to look at motherhood in a different light, even if only for a moment.

Goodness knows, if we've trudged through anything together and come out breathing, it's the admission that God is making us new. Every moment we ask for His wisdom. Every time we loosen our control, in every choice we make in every relationship or situation. I don't believe we need to be perfect, or superlative, or have it all. Because if there is anything *un*changing, it is the availability of God's divine wisdom, uniquely crafted just for you, waiting for your interest. For you to go somewhere quiet and seek. To brave that conversation and knock. To admit your own faults and ask Him to equip you.

What I pray that you and I have gently opened up is a new realization that God's voice may not be the loudest, but it's the one we need. His wisdom for us can come in any way, shape, or form, but I hope we're gracious enough with ourselves to receive it. Especially while we're offered the opportunity to help guide the next generation of souls. Remember, all of us are only living what's left of this life. It's time to start listening for your purpose while you can.

So when someone urges you to have it all, remember that *you have all you need by the grace of God.*

If you feel you have to do it all, remind yourself that *you can choose, God willing.*

Instead of trying to be it all, be thankful that *simply being you is furthering God's plan.*

And before you rush in to fix it all, lean

back into the wonder of *continual transformation without your orchestration.*

Now, go be the mom He made you to be. Apply the practices we've explored together in this book. Or, best of all, use the wisdom that only you are hearing to create your own brand of calm in the chaos.

We need you, just the way you are.

He Knows My Name

By Francesca Battistelli, Mia Feldes,
and Seth Mosley

I wouldn't choose me first if
I was looking for a champion
In fact, I'd understand if
You picked everyone before me
But that's just not my story
True to who You are
You saw my heart
And made
Something out of nothing

I don't need my name in lights
I'm famous in my Father's eyes
Make no mistake
He knows my name
I'm not living for applause
I'm already so adored
It's all His stage
He knows my name
He knows my name

acknowledgments

Thank you from the core of my soul to all the moms who make me brave. Without real moms Dionne to edit and inspire me, Heather to demonstrate calm, Mary Beth to help me laugh, Megan to be my guide, Mindy to exemplify love, and my own mom to encourage this book journey, read my manuscript versions, and offer insight—it would have remained a storm in my heart. You all are my blue sky and I love you so much.

Because of my mom, I have a fiercely passionate relationship with God, who blows my mind through the simplest things. I met him in the form of a tiny resin baby Jesus at the base of my childhood Christmas tree, and He captured my heart forever.

Moms who told me their truths are the reason I kept writing. Thank you for finding time in your busy lives to listen for wisdom with me. God is the reason I recognize your love. Love and thanks, also to Casey, my example to follow; and Katie, my spirited and fearless co-server; for your prayers and goodwill.

To my daughter, Mira; my son, Victor; and my husband, Barry—thank you for your faith that shapes me. When I didn't believe, you believed that God had something to whisper through me. You are why I finished this. You are why I want to begin every day.

about the author

Lia Martin received her degree in Mass Communications and graduated *cum laude* from Virginia Commonwealth University. A former assistant preschool teacher and former co-owner of a marketing and advertising agency, she now works as a freelance writer, specializing in blogs, videos, websites, scriptwriting, print publications, and more. Yet amid everything she does, Lia is most content with being a mom. She has learned her most important parenting lessons from raising two awesome teenagers, Mira and Victor, with her soulmate and husband, Barry Martin. The Martins live in Glen Allen, Virginia. Lia invites you to share your mom stories with her at www.LiaMartinWriting.com.

CPSIA information can be obtained
at www.ICGtesting.com
Printed in the USA
BVHW03s0148250918
528376BV00001B/23/P